JUST CALL ME FIERCE

Carol Townsend

Eph. 3:14-19

Just Call Me Fierce: Lessons from the Women of Luke

Copyright © 2023 Carol Townsend

This book is set in the typeface *Athelas* designed by Veronika Burian and Jose Scaglione.

Paperback ISBN: 979-8-85687-736-5

A Publication of *Tall Pine Books*
119 E Center Street, Suite B4A | Warsaw, Indiana 46580
www.tallpinebooks.com

| 1 23 23 20 16 02 |

Published in the United States of America

Just Call Me Fierce

LESSONS FROM THE WOMEN *of* LUKE

CAROL TOWNSEND

A LITANY TO HONOR WOMEN

We walk in the company of the women who have gone before, mothers of the faith both named and unnamed, ***testifying with ferocity and faith*** to the Spirit of wisdom and healing.

They are the judges, the prophets, the martyrs, the warriors, poets, lovers, and saints who are near to us in the shadow of awareness, in the crevices of memory, in the landscape of our dreams.

We walk in the company of Deborah, who judged the Israelites with authority and strength.

We walk in the company of Esther, who used her position as queen to ensure the welfare of her people.

We walk in the company of you whose names have been lost and silenced, who kept and cradled the wisdom of the ages.

We walk in the company of the woman with the flow of blood, who audaciously sought her healing and release.

We walk in the company of Mary Magdalene, who wept at the empty tomb until the risen Christ appeared.

We walk in the company of Phoebe, who led an early church in the empire of Rome.

We walk in the company of Perpetua of Carthage, whose witness in the third century led to her martyrdom.

We walk in the company of St. Christina the Astonishing, who resisted death with persistence and wonder.

We walk in the company of Julian of Norwich, who wed imagination and theology, proclaiming, "All shall be well."

We walk in the company of Sojourner Truth, who stood against oppression, righteously declaring in 1852, "Ain't I a woman!"

We walk in the company of the Argentine mothers of the Plaza de Mayo, who turned their grief to strength, standing together to remember "the disappeared" children of war with a holy indignation.

We walk in the company of Alice Walker, who named the lavender hue of womanish strength.

We walk in the company of you mothers of the faith, who teach us to resist evil with boldness, to lead with wisdom, and to heal.

*To my husband, Kirk and my daughter, Anna
for your steadfastness in the midst of my chaos.
You are my rocks, and I love you.*

*To my professor, Michael F. Bird,
for making me do this.*

Contents

INTRODUCTION

☙

WHEN I WAS 51 years old, I went to college. No, I didn't go back to college. I started college. As a freshman. I soon realized that even though this had never been part of my long-term goals, it was definitely a part of God's.

I had never contemplated a college degree. I was doing okay without it. I was a stay-at-home mom. I led women's Bible studies. I taught Bible classes for married couples. And it was fine until the day it wasn't. So, I found myself for the next seven years chipping away at all things theological, all while raising a middle schooler along with a supportive husband who did everything that I had to give up doing (praise the Lord, and bless his heart).

This academic journey of mine might seem a tad crazy to a lot of people and, believe me, I've heard it. Why would a wife and mom who has all of life's comforts, who could pretty much choose from a list of all things easy, leave it all and go to school? Why would I give up lazy days, luncheons, and vacations to sit in endless lectures about first-century scholars? Why would I spend time writing a ten-page paper on Old Testament Theology when I could be playing tennis? I think this book explains that journey because what I encourage you to do on these pages is exactly what school did for me. Those years of studying, writing, and conversing about higher things gave me confidence and reminded me that I was smart and that who I am is enough to do what God set out for me. I realized during my educational journey that I don't need to depend on anyone else to get done what God requires of me. It taught me that I need to stand up for myself. To trust my instincts. And to always, always keep moving forward.

Now, this was not my first foray into brave-land, and I knew God would guide and direct me through this process. And let me say here—He was beyond faithful. But it still wasn't easy. I cried over tests, papers sent my perfectionism into overdrive, failures made me sad, and then there was math! Math people: I adore you and thank you for keeping us on track but no...I mean, just no. Despite these challenges, I knew God had called me. There were even days that I shed tears of joy because I knew that I was exactly where God wanted me. I knew it was a God thing, even though I couldn't explain why I was there or where it was all leading. Even with our house flooding, having to rebuild it, and ultimately relocating to another city, I never missed a beat. I just got up and walked it every day for seven years. I graduated in 2018 with a Bachelor of Arts in Christianity. It was surreal, and I still return to the pictures from that day to relive it all just a little. My diploma has a special place in my office to remind me of God's faithfulness when He calls me to be bold.

I learned a lot but probably forgot even more on this journey. But what I came away with is this: *You have to be brave to walk with God.* If you want to be what your heart is telling you to be, then you must get up and move forward—even when you are not sure where you are going. You can't look around for a second. You can't compare your life with anyone else's, overthink what is ahead of you (which is my gift, based on what my family says), and you certainly can't justify why something else might be easier. Just about anything will be easier than what you are called to. God's purpose for you will never be about ease or comfort; it will simply be about trusting in the One who calls.

I have never considered myself to be brave and certainly not fierce. I always thought of myself as a pretty big chicken. Attempting to snow ski, holding on tightly as my husband exerts his need for speed on land or sea, and walking (or more like crawling) across extremely high suspension bridges are just a few things that come to mind in my chicken-dom. But in retrospect, I can now see in many instances in my life—and especially along my spiritual journey—just how brave I have been. For the most part, these times were accompanied by only a speck of faith while unknowingly being carried by Jesus Himself. It is not necessarily a very pretty journey or one I can boast about personally, but it is one that worked out simply because I took one step in the right direction with a desire to not live this life in vain and, of course, a boatload of God's grace. I came out with some scrapes and bruises and even questioned my sanity more than once (I mean a bunch), but this book is proof that, because of that said courage, I am exactly where I am supposed to be. One of the most important purposes of my brave journey is to now share it with you in the hope that you will step out in the same way.

I wrote this book for one reason—well, maybe two. The first one is: God used a professor to encourage me to write about the women of Luke based on a paper I had turned in. He pointed at me from across the room when he said it. God used this professor (one I had only known for five days) who seemed to know me better than I knew myself. It didn't take long for me to realize my purpose. I took it seriously. Secondly, and most importantly, I write it for you: my faith-seeking sister-in-Christ. I have often felt called in my life to encourage others simply because of what God has shown me along my journey. I believe without a doubt that my struggles—and even downright failures—have been, not only lessons for my own faith and life but upon arrival on solid ground, something valuable to be shared with others. God continually opens doors and leads me head-on to others who are struggling in the same way as I have and in need of what I had to learn the hard way. I wouldn't trade a minute of that rocky road for the sweet fruit it has provided.

So, what has God led me to say? I want to encourage you to embrace the calling God has for your life. I want to help you receive your courage. I want you to be brave enough to step up and out and past everyone else who is too afraid to do it. When my daughter was a toddler, God began impressing upon me to pray these words: "If everyone goes west, make me brave enough to take her east, if that is where you need her to be." Think like that.

In this study, I will begin by providing the background story of the Old Testament that leads to the eternal redemption of God's people. We will build upon that foundation, leading to the fierce women of Luke, whose lives were forever changed by the life and ministry of Jesus. As I do in my own biblical study, I encourage you to keep a daily journal of pertinent scripture, spiritual encouragement and enlightenment, and any personal convictions or challenges that you may be led to. This is so helpful as we build on our knowledge and understanding of God and especially of ourselves that ultimately will lead to our purpose in God's kingdom work. You will also find at the end of each chapter a "Time of Reflection" that will help you in your faith walk by digging deeper into who God created you to be. I have also included a biblical prayer as well as a personal prayer to aid in seeking wisdom in your spiritual walk. You will find resources at the end of the book for understanding God's purpose and plan more deeply and will hopefully lead you into meaningful biblical study and heartfelt worship.

My hope is that you will begin a deep spiritual search of finding your true identity in Christ. I want you to be able to ask yourself hard questions in the hopes of grasping all things eternal. This is meant to guide you into making your life count as a child of God as you put His creation purposes ahead of your daily existence. It is to help you become intentional about finding your spiritual call in a way that enables others to do the same. It is now time to step into the fierce faith that awaits you—to move toward what your mind and heart say are yours for the taking. Let's start to believe in the you that God created you to be and the gifts that He so generously gave you.

CHAPTER ONE

ON BEING FIERCE

Ꮛ᎒

SEVERAL YEARS AGO, my daughter's friend used a word to describe a particular outfit I was wearing. It was very complimentary, especially for a middle-aged woman, but for the life of me, I could never remember what it was. Every so often I would ask her what it was he called me, and one day she exasperatedly replied, "Mom, you need to write that down." So I did. It was fierce.

My journey with fierceness began long before I actually believed I had any in me. God has been preparing me for this road for some time and the true meaning of this sweet compliment has become more deeply rooted than my exterior wardrobe. I have realized that the weakness that has been revealed in me was not the person God had created but what I allowed myself to believe. Underneath it all was determination, perseverance, and consistent faith. Whether they be great or small, they were routinely called to the surface. I learned that my fierceness was not an over-confidence of self or ability, an overpowering of any given situation, or loudness of being but actually one of complete surrender and vulnerability at the feet of my Savior who has showered me with any and all things needed to be used by Him and for Him.

So I write to women who are comfortable in their world but yet sense something more bubbling under the surface. Those that seem to have it all yet feel something is amiss. I write to encourage believers of all seasons to begin to look deep into your own hearts and seek the greater things that God has intended for you. The things that call for sacrifice and surrender that come from knowing you are all God created you to be. Not for simply your own spiritual advancement but because you deeply desire the sustenance of the eternal things of God. This is for believers who are banking on their spiritualness, busyness, and likeability to confirm their faith and not on developing their actual Christ-likeness. A likeness that only comes from a committed relationship that loves and serves the One who came to love and serve. I hope this study will encourage women to turn their passion from the temporal things of this world and begin to seek a fierce faith that calls them to a closer walk with God.

Before we dive into the women of Luke, I find it important to talk about what it is we are seeking to become and what that will look like in the physical world. While searching for the definition of fierce, it took me on many routes but ultimately three clear meanings that were easily sifted through. "Ferocious aggressiveness" and "powerful and destructive" were undoubtedly *not* what God was talking about when He redeemed us and called us to discipleship. But the third one resonated with all things Christ-like. I found that "heartfelt and powerful intensity" best resembled this fierceness as it pertains to the divine grace and call of God that leads to all things eternal. This results in living with the bold confidence that life is far more than our simple existence but is measured by the holy standards set apart for us from the beginning of creation.

As believers, we are given basic abilities that reveal this type of intensity in our relationship to the One who uses us for His kingdom purposes. As Apostle Paul tells us in Romans 8:28, we are *called* because of God's great love and mercy that has been displayed throughout salvation history. We have also been *equipped* for all good things that relate to Him through our belief in Jesus

Christ's death and resurrection (2 Timothy 3:17). And Jesus Himself spoke directly to His apostles when He promised the *empowerment* of the Holy Spirit to work the will of God in and through us (Acts 1:8). As we walk alongside these fierce women of Luke, we will see these essential abilities come to life through their faith and humble service. We can sit at their feet as we watch their lives be supernaturally changed by the simple touch of Jesus' hand, His compelling word, and their confidence arise in His undeniable mission to save His Father's creation. These women were restored, not only physically, but to a life lived out solely for His purposes as humble servants, demonstrating to us exactly what it takes to become fierce warriors for the mission of Jesus Christ.

The following are three factors common to our faith walk and exhibited by the women of Luke that kept them in step with their Savior on their spiritual journey.

DETERMINATION

Those we encounter in this study, Elizabeth and Mary, those healed by His touch, the women who followed Jesus, all opened up their lives to Him with a *determination* that began with sincere faith and worship of Him as their Savior. A decision made with their hearts and minds that changed their path forever. They decided to follow Jesus, and as the old hymn states, there would be no turning back. These women show us that when you come face to face with Jesus, your purpose in this world is changed. Your mindset and your heart are renewed. Your road narrows and your direction is singularly focused. Isaiah 50:7 promises that *"because the Sovereign Lord helps me, I will not be disgraced. Therefore, I have set my face like flint, and I know that I will not be put to shame."* Luke shows the women as supernaturally changed: the weight of the world had left them; through seeking and following Jesus they now were drawing strength from His very words, and as Isaiah states, they too were like flint. Flint is a very hard, immovable, unchangeable stone that is actually used to make tools that break moveable, changeable stone. It is steel in rock form. Like the psalmist proclaims, *"God is in the midst of her; she shall not be moved"* (96:4-6). Apostle Paul writes in Acts 20:24 that even as he faced prison, *"none of these things move me."* Having put aside the world and its uncertainties, these women were balanced on the solid rock of Jesus' mission and were unmovable in their faithfulness to Him.

Luke 9:51 states that Jesus also *"set his face to Jerusalem."* Jesus made a decision for His Father's purpose. He performed great miracles and spoke truth to falsehood. He lifted up the least and the lost and called out the rich and powerful, but what He came to do was to die for sinners. He set His mind on it. He knew it must be done, and He, the Son of Man and the Son of God, was the only One for the job. Beyond all obstacles, fear, and threats,

He walked right into it for the glory of God, prepared to show the Father's great love to His people. These statements reveal to us as believers and fellow heirs in God's family that we, too, must be determined in our walk with Him as He prepares and provides for us throughout the journey. Empowered by that great love and encouraged by His continuing faithfulness, we must believe that it is *"all good"* just as God declared while speaking creation into being. We are to set our minds on the greater things and be determined to finish the race because we trust that God is with us, providing the way.

I think one of the most serious things that stall our spiritual journey is shame. The prophet Isaiah (50:7) is confident in his words that because of our faithfulness and obedience, we will not be disgraced (forgotten, forsaken, humiliated, or left out). What the Old Testament prophet spoke over the nation of Israel is ours to claim and walk in assurance today. Jesus' sacrifice comes to clear our past and wash His sweet purification over those bewildering days of old. Throughout the book of Isaiah's overwhelming visual of God and all of His glory, the prophet shows the purpose of replacing our rags with *"garments of salvation and robes of righteousness."* This is such a beautiful rendering of what God sees when He looks down upon His faithful believers. It is such encouragement for those moments of our past that cause us to shiver at the things we have seen and done that are far from godliness. But once we begin to see ourselves adorned in all the glory we were created for, those memories will fade far into the background, and you will realize that the sinful person of old was never really you to begin with. The real you has been freed and is now in right standing with the Father in heaven, the Redeemer, and your Redeemer. Like Paul exhorts in 2 Corinthians 5:17, *"the old is gone, and the new is here!"* Our sin is heartbreaking, but our Savior is forever faithful to forgive and always forget. This means we can too.

Read these extra verses about shame and forgiveness:

Psalm 34:4-5 The faithful are never covered with shame.

Psalm 103:2-4 The Lord forgives all, heals all, redeems, and crowns us with His love.

Isaiah 54:4-7 You will forget the shame of your youth and remember no more.

Romans 5:1 We are at peace with God through Jesus Christ.

2 Peter 3:9 God is patient, not wanting anyone to perish but everyone to come to repentance.

In our spiritual journey, there is no room or occasion for lukewarm. It benefits none to walk slightly with Jesus.

Any level of intensity in our faith is powerful enough to continually propel us forward and deeper into wisdom and understanding. Empowering us to fearlessly seek out the next step in our path, knowing that what our Savior began in this world and in us, He is faithful to complete. Always growing, always learning, always seeking to know more. Paul encourages us to *"work out our salvation in reverence and fear . . . in a world full of crooked and perverse people"* (Phil. 2:12-15). Even in Paul's day, the world was much like what we are experiencing in the 21st century. Evil seems to reign at every turn, and its divisive measures are a tough battle to fight. It is easy to get caught up in the ideas and opinions swirling around us. Our confidence and comfort are shaken at every morsel of worldly news, and our hearts race at the plight of those living in defeated lands, leading us to fear that could one day be our fate. And, truthfully, it could. But when our foundation is laid firmly and solely on the grander picture, the eternal picture, of the plan laid out as God's people for God's purpose, then we can look past those grim images to joy-filled days that introduce us to the true life awaiting us.

Even in the midst of this darkness, we have the opportunity to stand in awe of our great God. To lean into the supernatural aspects of our Creator who sent His Son to redeem us because, simply enough, He loves us. We can rest in the remembrance of what He has done for His people as a whole and what He has done for each of us personally, connecting the dots of our story that brings an understanding of His mission. An understanding that includes the history of His character in the stories of the Old Testament that opens up the doors of His fulfillment and revelation of the New. Always trusting that what our great God began in us and in this world, He is faithful to complete (Phil 1:6).

Walking in this life with Jesus keeps us on one side: the winning side. In Matthew 10:34, Jesus says, "I did not come to bring peace, but a sword." The line has been drawn in the sand. Jesus is either first or He is not at all. The fear of the things of this world subsides when I remind myself that we win in the end. Actually, the battle has already been won. Jesus' death was our victory, and Revelation 21 promises that it is all being made new and ours to inherit. It might get ugly before it gets beautiful, but oh, how beautiful it will be.

We will see in the coming chapters, that after meeting Jesus, these women lined their lives up with the winning team. With the Father's will. They founded their life on their Creator God who sent His Son to redeem His people from this fallen world because of His great love for us. Fierce faith, like the women of Luke, will cause you to move the movable and change the changeable as all disciples were called to do. Their determination led them straight to Him and their humble faith was enhanced by their *heartfelt and powerful intensity* for the mission of Jesus Christ.

PERSEVERANCE

It's easy to persevere when we know where we are going, but true wisdom and understanding come when we are led by the Spirit down the dark winding roads. These roads may cause us to condemn our own existence, but in the end, our persistence will lead us to all things everlasting. Perseverance doesn't just keep us moving; it teaches us why our movement matters and it brings out the roadblocks from within. The more we move toward God, the more we move away from the things that dim the view. For me, dwelling on the negatives of my past is something that has always led me to doubt and frustration, not to mention a load of shame and guilt. But as I was led to more constructive and pure thoughts, I found that forgiveness and gratefulness were necessary in gaining stable and positive ground. Forgiveness of the pain caused by others and of self is a great release from the old and gives us the freedom to let go of the things encumbering and distracting us from the new. We have all heard that forgiveness is more about yourself than the other person but it is for sure twofold. Yes, forgiveness is healing to our soul and self, but when we forgive others, we can shake off the need to control our circumstances and those involved, and we can rest in the land of complete reliance on the One who knows what is best. Yes and Amen (sigh of relief here). We have freed them (and ourselves) to let God do what God needs to do while we keep pushing forward. Then in spiritual clarity, gratitude flows out because we finally conclude that all things work together for good. His good. My good. Everyone's good. He broke the chains so that we can be grateful that freedom from all things worldly is a possibility and as Psalm 96:4-6 encourages, "He is worthy to be praised and deserves a thousand hallelujahs." Gratefulness, yes gratefulness. Now and forever and a thousand things in between.

While we are talking about moving past things that block our view, I feel it is important to add suffering and sorrow into the mix. As Christians, suffering alarms us because many of us are seeking the blessing, not the discipline. But how can it be that while we are just trying to climb to the top of this thing called spiritual life, someone goes and turns off the lights? Romans 5:3-5 reveals that not only can we boast in God and all His glory, but we can also find glory in our sufferings. Wait, what? Suffering? That does not sound like fun. Who wants to suffer? Aren't we praying for God to make things all good? Don't we want all that bad stuff to go away? Isn't that why we trust in Him, pray, and go to church? So we can be good Christians? The answer to all of these is a resounding no. Paul's story demonstrates that suffering produces in us what we are supposed to be. Suffering keeps our eyes on Jesus, who brings us through better off. I have suffered through many things in my life. Some I can blame on others, a lot I can blame on myself, but all in all, it's when I turned my face to God and asked "What now?" that the lighted road to my purpose began to slowly be revealed. Apostle Paul teaches us through his own experience of suffering. He knew that suffering leads to *perseverance, builds character, and gives hope* in our sovereign Lord, who knows exactly who we are and exactly what we need. I can now look back and see that what I thought was breaking me was actually giving me life, and I would not change a minute of it. In my weakness, my pleas, my mourning, I was strengthened and encouraged to continue, to carry on, focused on the journey that continually leads to the eternal things that are being perfected in time. Pushing through adversity, obstacles, rejection, and sorrow, knowing that the battle engulfing my fierce faith is not won by aggression or by might, but by a steadfast longing to be the conqueror I am called to be. Now, please know, that we all have differing levels of suffering: people hurt us, we hurt ourselves, and then there is the broken world in which we live, and bad things just happen. God is not always teaching us in our suffering. Sometimes He just holds us in His hands. Nothing to learn here but that He loves us and totally relates to our loss.

As we let go of the things that haunt us and keep in step with God's perfecting of our holiness, Jesus becomes our story: past, present, and future. The light begins to shine on His great purpose for us, and His strength begins to conquer that wayward nature. As Paul writes of his personal conversion in Acts 26, he was *"overpowered"* by God on the road to Damascus, which had left him blind. He tells this story in remembrance of the dark life he lived in his pursuit and persecution of new believers. In the light, he remembered the things of the past in order to better express who he was in the present as a newly appointed *"minister and witness,"* testifying only to *"Jesus Christ and Him Crucified."* In the same way, the women of Luke found themselves on the bleak streets of uncertainty. Living diligently on their daily journey until something stopped them in their tracks. A special delivery that will change the world. A transformative touch that renewed their life. A call to worship in a whole new way. Armed with child-like faith and jubilant hearts, they each rushed forward to the pinhole of light as God drew back the curtains to show exactly what Paul had witnessed: the purpose of it all.

The lesson here is the same for everyone: He is with us and for us and has us in the palm of His hand, and there is always hope. In a world full of letdowns and dead-end roads, God promises that hope in Him never disappoints. We can move forward in that hope, knowing there is a much grander picture and that, as His children, we have everything we need to complete this journey with heads held high. The light is shining in the dark even when we don't see it. So persevere, my friends. Your fierce is showing because of your heartfelt and powerful intensity in your own personal walk with Jesus. Because with Him, the result and reward will always outweigh any adversity that comes your way.

CONSISTENCY

Let us also be reminded that our walk revolves around *consistency*. This doesn't mean we never fail and err in our ways. Fierce faith is not about how many times you drop the ball but about staying in the game. It is not about how many times you doubt the process, the call, or your own abilities, but it's about trusting God at His word. It is not about comparing yourself to anyone else but remembering who you are in Christ and what He has personally created you to be. It is being consistent in your desire for Jesus. Dependent on the Holy Spirit to guide us as John 15:4 instructs us to *"abide in Him as he also abides in us."* The word abide means *to remain*. He is constant, never leaving or forsaking His children. As His faithful children, He is asking for us to do the same for Him.

First Peter 2:1 calls us to get rid of anything in us that does not honor God, to *"crave"* spiritual instruction and direction, and to *"grow up"* in our salvation. I have been in church all my life, studied and taught God's Word for 25 years, and even got a degree in Christianity, and I am still growing up. Because I still sin. Sometimes my flesh gets the best of me. Fear of the unknown in the days ahead can be paralyzing. Negative thoughts can interrupt any peaceful moment of any day. I think the wrong things, say the wrong things, desire the wrong things. But I consistently take it back to the cross, where it all started, and lay it back down. The more I do that, the less I have to. The more consistent you are in your craving for Jesus, the less you will want what doesn't honor Him. Jesus didn't have to consistently die for us. He died once. He took all of what Adam introduced to the world and demolished it on the cross, once and for all. Sin has been conquered. It no longer rules the world, so we are no longer rocked by the waves of temptation. We can stand back up and take hold of what has been given to us. A new life and victory in it.

Keep in mind that regardless of your age, your circumstances, in blessing or in defeat, be *determined, persevering,* and *consistent* in your faith. Stay the course, pushing past the obstacles, remaining steadfast, and abounding in the purposes of the Lord. You were created for this moment and called to those purposes. Keep in fierce faith with a heartfelt and powerful intensity in your devotion to Jesus Christ, your Lord and your Savior, who *ALWAYS* has a heartfelt and powerful intensity in His devotion to you.

TIME OF REFLECTION

- Do I know I am saved through Christ's death and resurrection? How? What age? Who led you to the Lord?
- Have I asked for forgiveness of my sins? Am I aware of my weaknesses and the sins that draw me away from the Lord?
- Have I forgiven those who have hurt me or those who I have something against? Do I have unforgiveness or bitterness in my heart for anyone? Who? Why?
- Where do I place my identity/security? My past? My accomplishments and possessions? My children? My husband?
- What do I fear? What is hard to let go of? What am I trying to control?
- What are my gifts? My abilities/strengths? What would I like to share about myself and my faith with the world?
- Have you ever shared the gospel with someone? Not your experience or a sermon you heard but the straight-up story of Jesus' death and resurrection.

SCRIPTURAL PRAYER: *We continually ask God to fill you with the knowledge of his will through all the wisdom and understanding that the Spirit gives, so that you may live a life worthy of the Lord and please him in every way: bearing fruit in every good work, growing in the knowledge of God, being strengthened with all power according to his glorious might so that you may have great endurance and patience, and giving joyful thanks to the Father, who has qualified you to share in the inheritance of his holy people in the kingdom of light. For he has rescued us from the dominion of darkness and brought us into the kingdom of the Son he loves, in whom we have redemption, the forgiveness of sins. (Colossians 1:9-14)*

PERSONAL PRAYER: *I come to You today to give You my heart and my life. I ask You to forgive me of my sins and to lead me onto Your righteous path. Beginning today, Lord, I surrender all that I am and all that I will become to You. Align my mind, my heart, and my actions with Your will and Your ways so that I may be a testimony to Your life, death, and resurrection. Help me to be a witness and a holy priest to those around me so that I not only glorify Your name but lead others to eternal life. I ask for wisdom and discernment in matters of Your Word and of my calling so that I know that I am pleasing to You and adding to Your kingdom. Thank You for all that You have done in my life and for loving me as Your child. Amen.*

CHAPTER TWO

THIS IS US

ॐ

I HAVE AN amazing gift of focusing on myself. Who am I? Why am I here? What is the purpose of it all? These are common themes ringing through my head. I am one of those people who needs to know the answers. I can waste a lot of time trying to figure it all out. For example, in the first few moments upon the death of my 96 year old mother, I frantically tried to wrap my tiny brain around where her soul was directly following her passing. I wanted to know. I even asked shamelessly, "Billions of people have passed away, Lord. Where are they? Where do you keep them until Your return?" I actually might have even said, "store them." It was purely informational. Now that may sound more like a six-year-old than a 60-year-old Bible-teaching Christianity major, but I felt I needed to know, even deserved to know, the details. I mean, it was my mother after all. Frankly, I was actually shocked that this is where I went directly following her death. I had never worried about it or talked to her about it. She was a believer, and I knew where she was going, but honestly, letting her go was a completely different story. As Christians, we live in the present, banking on the future of eternal life, but when we are faced with it, especially when it's our mother, our feelings get a little warped. My need for details was honestly a lesson in trust that I obviously needed to work on. When the supernatural and reality meet, it brings out any loopholes that might have not been worked on. I guess it was time for me to do that.

Fortunately, I am blessed with very matter-of-fact friends who willingly yell scripture at me when I go to these places of doubt. All I heard from across the phone line was, "2 Corinthians 5:8" when I shared my concern for her whereabouts. "Gone from the body, present with the Lord," my dear friend reprimanded me, "that's all you need to know!" There it is. The difference between self and truth is evident in this story. When I rely on my own common sense and depend on the facts of a situation, I wander off into a no man's land of fear and doubt. But when I am shaken back into the reality of who I am and to whom I belong, well, I no longer need to see things so concretely. I can trust in the Word of the God who saved me through His Son and rest in the grander picture beyond this tiny little world. Doubt will always find its place somewhere in my life, but knowing who I am in Christ always leads me back to solid ground, and I will always find rest in that land.

Many years ago, I was fortunate enough to discover the importance of the ancient stories of the Old Testament. It began in my first Bible Study Fellowship class in the study of Moses. Of course, I knew who Moses was along with many biblical heroes that my young life in Sunday school had taught, but little did I know the power these stories possessed. Yes, the New Testament holds the key to Jesus' accomplishment of what the Father set into motion, but knowing who God was from the beginning is instrumental in knowing who He is and is to come. The knowledge I gained from these Old Testament studies set my spiritual life and calling into motion. As I walked through the lives of these ancient patriarchs and historical events, I felt the pieces come together, making sense of it all. It had purpose from the first days of creation throughout history and way before the modern centuries came to light. Looking back and beyond the arrival of our Savior, I found a well-worn path that began with God's eternal love for His creative order. I waded through every kept promise and delivered covenant, and I marveled at His unequaled patience as He guided His people to holiness. One important thing that the Old Testament history taught me was how badly mankind needed to be saved, which helped me finally make sense of my own sinful nature. Knowing God's story from creation onward is the foundation where I find consistent rest for my weakness and solid ground for my ever-growing faith.

Although many first-century Israelites witnessed by sight or by word the occasion of Jesus' life on earth, I was beyond blessed to pull back the curtain on the full account of this supernatural event that gave me the ability to find the personal meaning behind it. These blessings begin by acknowledgement that the biblical authors who share these historical, literal, and allegorical narratives have been ordained by the Spirit to reveal the events that lead to the true purpose of this story (See 2 Timothy 3:16-17). These ancient narratives clearly showed me not only who the Creator God is and His desire for His people but that the invitation extends to all who seek membership into this restorative journey back to garden fellowship. The great news is that as believers we now have the opportunity to live as if we are already there. The kingdom of God is here. We have been delivered by our Savior, and we can now live life to its fullest. We no longer have to ask, "Why me?" but instead, "What of me?" What is my place in this kingdom? How can I be used? What of me, Lord?

To find our true identity, we must first remove all the worldly adjectives that we have attached ourselves to and let all that Jesus was, is, and is to come, begin to fill that void. This is truly who you are and why you are here. So let's mentally prepare ourselves to begin this journey with a desire to break down some walls and open up to all that has been given to us. The rest of this book will be meaningless without the power that comes with making this life-changing decision of finding and knowing your identity in Christ. To understand this is to know the One who created you and redeemed you. There are numerous accounts, Old and New Testament alike, that explain this phenomenon of self. Myself. Yourself. And the common ground we share. This week's chapter is solely for the purpose of you knowing you. We all have differing characteristics, personalities, and desires. We all come from different family backgrounds, upbringings, and economic status. But what if I told you that we all have one amazing thing in common: In Jesus we are all exactly the same. To understand this is to know the One who created you and redeemed you.

IN HIS IMAGE

The foundation begins in Genesis 1 with God's created order and the purpose behind it and should be the glue that holds this entire story together. Believing that God is the creator of this universe and every living thing in it should be the driving force behind our trust in all He has planned and has done in it. In one short statement beginning in verse 26, God bestows His first covenant with mankind as He creates them in His image *so that* they may rule over every living thing. His purpose is clear that, along with having fellowship with Him, we have been entrusted as His official co-creators. Our responsibilities become clearer in the following verses when God tells Adam and Eve to "be fruitful and increase, fill the earth and subdue it, and again rule over it." So if we break this down, God has created us with His own intellect and ability to take control of the helm. What He had just accomplished by creating, increasing, and reigning over, He is now sending His people to go and do the same. Now let's be clear, we are not called to be reminders of who God is but instead faithful representatives of His loving and merciful nature who seek to continue to create, fill, and maintain the purposes of God's kingdom throughout this world He created.

So how does this work? First, we have the ability to be fruitful and to increase, not just in population, but in all that He gives us. To nurture, grow, and bring increase to any and all things that will bring glory to Him and bring growth to the community of believers. This is a call to take our eyes solely off ourselves while opening the doors for others to dwell in the halls of His kingdom. To share ourselves, our gifts, our blessings in order to comfort, bring hope, and to bless others as we have been blessed. To enlarge the hearts and minds of those set before us so that they are positioned to do the same. A continual circle of love, hope, and faith that abounds from one to another as we grow and fellowship together as children of God.

We also have the ability to "subdue" the earth. The word subdue means to "get the better of." This beautiful thing called planet earth is ours to be enjoyed as well as to be conquered. It is our job to replenish, restore, and build upon it in a way that fits within God's will. To work with the natural things that will show our gratefulness by returning the glory back to the Giver. This glorious earth is ours to manage as the gift that it is, and we have been given the right to rule it. Not dictate, intimidate, or abuse, but know that we have been set apart for the goodness of all of these things. Just as God separated the water from the land and the dark from the light, as human beings we have been set apart from all living things to cherish, protect, and have dominion over it. In the last verses of Genesis 1, we are told that God has given us "everything." Every living thing. We have His nature, and we have all things. This was God's way of giving His people fierce faith from the get-go. We have been given everything we need to continue God's work. To do these things, we must first agree with our loving Creator that we belong to this order, have a purpose in His kingdom, and a place in this story, along with having an innate ability to continue His mission of creation. *We were meant for this.*

Read Isaiah 61 to reiterate what Christ did to reclaim you as God's image bearers.

AFTER THE FALL

After the ultimate exile from the garden, God's image in mankind was scarred by the sinful nature that had entered through Adam. But because we serve a loving and faithful God, He began something new. Genesis 9 gives us a look into the genealogical well from which God's futuristic plans flow. Abraham will be given the honors as the father of the chosen nation of Israel in God's continuing covenant with His people. Wanting a people for Himself that would be a light to all nations, and a blessing to all generations while representing, once again, His image to the world around them. Israel would be the beacon that would reveal the one true God to the world. God begins His atonement provision in the wilderness tabernacle that would present His people holy before Him. In disrupting the sin that divided God from His people, He would achieve the long-lost fellowship once enjoyed in the garden. But this was only a temporary solution that would hopefully lead them to the understanding and acceptance of the finality of Jesus' sacrifice. But even after all they were given—the leaders, the law, and the land—their own human limitations interrupted God's plan, and they were exiled from the land once again. *This was us.*

This loss of identity that Israel suffered ultimately showed that they would need more than the tangible to be fully restored back to God's image. In Jesus, the gospels tell us, the provision was fulfilled. Jesus' own words of this fulfillment in the Sermon on the Mount in Matthew 5:17 reveal His purpose in bringing the final and everlasting covenant to His people. Our divine God came in human form through Jesus to show us not only what we needed, but that He was the only One who could fill that void. Not a savior to bring about military power or global status for this ancient community but one that came as a humble servant to take the wrath for our sins. A once and for all sacrifice.

God's eternal plan for mankind is revealed in His Son, Jesus Christ, who came to do for us what we could not do for ourselves. God sent His perfect image to us to fulfill and replace what was lost in the garden. Through Jesus, God restored mankind back to Himself for all of eternity. Jesus was a gift from God to His people and, like all gifts, must be received to be enjoyed. In Acts 26:18, Paul shares his own spiritual conversion and repentance when he tells of how God sent him "to open their eyes so that they may *receive* the forgiveness of sin." Because Paul's eyes were opened to his own need for forgiveness through Jesus Christ, someone he had fervently contested, he was now called to share this same gift. Because of this newfound faith, he was *given the ability* to turn from his sin and profess Jesus as the Messiah. This shows that it is not up to us to be better or different, but by simply receiving Jesus as our Savior, we automatically are. *This is us.*

NEW AND IMPROVED

In 2 Corinthians 5:17, Apostle Paul continues to teach the new church of the arrival of this "new creation" created by those of faith in Jesus Christ. This old self, new self attitude is the foundation of who we are and who we were meant to be. But first, we must deal with the old. We have been told all of our lives that our sins are forgiven and being the self-aware people that we are, we think about our own sins. Which we should. It is about our sin. But what if we thought about it in terms of just *SIN*? *SIN* as a whole. As the Son of Man, Jesus died for *ALL SIN*. Crucified it once and for all. He took *ALL* of its power, its destruction, its darkness, its promise of death to the cross. All of it. Romans 5:17 sums it up: "For if, because of one man's trespass, death reigned through one man (Adam). . . how much more will those who receive the abundance of grace and righteousness reign in life through the one man Jesus Christ." In other words, what Adam brought into the world, Jesus came to remove.

On the cross, the agony of the physical pain is hard to imagine but it is amplified by the separation He experienced from His holy Father because of our *SIN* on Him. This shows us what sin does. It strips us of everything we were intended to be. Adam and Eve immediately lost their freedom to be themselves because they chose to sin. They were immediately ashamed. They tried to cover up their story and their bodies. They hid from God. The garden story shows us how sin interrupted God's glorious creation of *US*. But Jesus changed all that by becoming like us and taking the burden of sin off the world. He cleared the way so that we might become what God meant for us to be. Through repentance, we convey our own sense of inability to change ourselves. We acknowledge our own lack and neediness. As hard as we try, we can never be what we were meant to be. Being good will grow tiresome and will only be felt skin deep. Repentance allows re-birth and is the evidence of our willingness to let go of all things that pertain to ourselves, our life, and this world, allowing God full access to our hearts and minds and bringing the cleansing we so need. Our conscious humbling and repentance before God opens the doors to the new creation and the new self. We can now receive this garden-intended freedom and fellowship that was meant for us from the beginning.

Read Romans 5:18; 1 Corinthians 5:21; Romans 5:6; Romans 8:1

God not only provided a way out; He provided a way forward. Jesus defeated sin through His death on the cross but that was not the end. It was the beginning. Our story continues in Romans 6:5 when Paul writes, "For if we have been united with him in a death like his, we will certainly also be united with him in a resurrection like his." If in faith we believe that Jesus took our sins in His death, then we must also agree that He also gave us new life. If I believe He died for my sin and defeated the death it promises, then I must believe He rose again. Otherwise, I am still left in my sin and have no good news to share. The resurrection is my hope because Jesus is with the Father reigning over my life, forgiving me, and restoring me to a new and better life continually. And even after all of this, He hasn't left us alone here to hope for the best. In Acts 2, Luke gives the story of the Holy Spirit's arrival after Jesus' ascension. The pouring out onto believers at Pentecost gave spiritual empowerment specifically to preach the gospel "to the ends of the earth." We have this resurrecting power to be and do all that God calls and wills in our life. John 14:20 promises that "on that day (of the Spirit's arrival), you will realize that I am in my Father, and you are in me, and I am in you" empowering us to live out His will in our daily life. This confirms the united front we possess as believers that keeps us moving on the short and narrow path. Keeping our eyes focused on God's perfect and peace-filled plan. As faithful believers, we are reigning with Him, once again. Because we are in Him and He is in us, we have been reunited to the image of God and fully restored with the ability to increase, manage, and rule over His creation.

Read 1 Corinthians 6:11, 15:17; John 1:1; Galatians 3:26-29; Ephesians 1:3

Since the beginning of time, man has been trying to conquer this world. From wealth, health, and joy-seeking we have all tried to find our place and our person in an attempt to make the most of this thing called life. If only we can build the white picket fence and check all the boxes, then we can leave this world in peace. Blessed. Healthy. Happy. But in knowing the person we were created to be and for the purpose we were created, we have to begin to look at things a little differently. This life is a spiritual journey that begins with knowing that we were made by God, for God. It is time to start seeing ourselves as important players in God's re-creation and of a much greater story. We must begin to seek our true purpose and identity that is only found within these walls.

TIME OF REFLECTION

- After studying the scripture from these last two weeks, what better understanding do you have of your salvation and God's purpose for your life?
- What stood out to you this week that you had never considered before?
- How will that change the way you live, think, work, parent...?
- Where in your life should you apply who you are in Christ instead of who you think you are in this world? What idols have you placed before God or sought comfort in?
- What strongholds or sins has God made you aware of that are keeping you from being completely His?
- Who have you chosen to forgive and asked to forgive you?
- What specifics are you asking God to change in your life? In yourself? In your circumstances?
- Have you repented of your sin and asked Jesus into your life?

SCRIPTURAL PRAYER: *Our Father in heaven, hallowed be your name, your kingdom come, your will be done, on earth as it is in heaven. Give us today our daily bread. And forgive us our debts, as we also have forgiven our debtors. And lead us not into temptation, but deliver us from the evil one. (Matthew 6:9 and Luke 11:2, Jesus instructs the community of believers how to pray)*

PERSONAL PRAYER: *Our Father in Heaven, thank You for dying for my sin and for making me a new creation. I am Yours, an heir to all things of Jesus, adopted into Your royal family, loved beyond measure, awaiting in hope of the day You return for those fierce in their faith. Keep me in Your hands and cause me to be obedient to Your ways and Your will for my life. I ask for a happy life. One where my feet are anchored on holy ground and my eyes are always lifted to You. Make me a light unto Your kingdom. May I become what You created me to be more and more each day.* Amen.

CHAPTER THREE

THE FOUNDATION OF FIERCE

❧

B EFORE WE START with the fierce women of Luke, we must first look at the original coura- geous acts that came before and what part they play in God's great kingdom story. For starters, know this: it has always been and still is all about the *land*. Since Genesis 1, biblical authors have been referencing this in some shape or form because it is the driving force behind God's creative purposes. The Old Testament sto- ries are not just about God's people and the occupation of a particular land in a particular time. It is an offering to all believers that began in the garden and leads us to His eternal kingdom.

ALL ABOUT THE LAND

Starting with the creation narrative, we are shown God's beginning purpose of fellowship with His created order happening on a special and unique piece of property. As the first tribal unit, Adam and Eve basically had the world by the tail but ultimately lost their grip after disobeying God's order. This tangible acreage that was theirs for the taking was set apart and created for God's people and filled with everything that they could possibly need or want. Comforts and delights that continually filled any possible void and banished any type of discomfort before it could ever take root. God gave dominion to man over this land, to care for it and nurture the things belonging to it, along with stipulations to sustain divine order. Basically calling them to keep their eyes on what God had provided and off of what is not theirs for the taking. This rule still applies.

As we move forward through the Old Testament, the land continues to be the main focus as God remains faithful to His covenant with Abraham as well as to Moses, the human vehicle that rescued His people out of slavery and moved them toward the promised land. It had been 650 years since that day of God's covenant with Abraham and 400 years since Israel was in captivity in Egypt. Both

Abraham's name and Israel's proportions had greatly increased as promised. Last but not least, God's promise to the father of this great nation is the *land*. Enter Joshua. He has been trained, served, and walked alongside Moses, believed in the covenant of Abraham, and is ready to fulfill the final quest of God's covenant and call for His people.

Find these stories in Genesis 12, 15, 17 and Exodus 6, 12

These courageous biblical saints questioned God a lot, doubted their worthiness, and feared the outcome of their appointment, not to mention they both hit some roadblocks along the way. The bravery and persistence of these men and the people that followed are undeniable, but it is Joshua who stands out in these narratives simply because God expressed personally to him that now is the time to "be strong and courageous." Today is the day that God's people are about to enter *the land*. The land of Canaan, set apart for the nation of Israel. The people promised to Abraham, led and re-led through the wilderness by Moses. But on this day, Joshua will take the honors.

After Moses' death, God commissioned Joshua with these famous words: "Be strong and courageous (fierce) for you will bring the Israelites into the land I promised them on oath (Abraham's covenant) and I myself will be with you." Brave faith is not needed; it is required. Joshua is a pure and unfettered example of fierceness and takes being brave to a whole new level. With the belief that the land was filled with giants and fortified walls, an opposition others believed to be unconquerable, Joshua marched in armed for battle, founded on a strength that came solely from his faith in the Word of God. Moses promised the people that the LORD would go before them and would never leave or forsake them. Joshua believed that and walked in and took what was his for the taking. That is fierce. That is faith. It has been and will always be about courageously taking the land. Joshua shows us how it is done and yes, it applies to us today.

Find these stories in Numbers 13-21 and Deuteronomy 29-31

Joshua's courageous story shows us three very important things about our land. He shows us how to take the land and receive what is already ours. We also are shown how to stay in that land. What tools we will need to plant our feet on solid ground and remain in that place no matter what draws us in another direction. Finally, Joshua shows how to take cover in order to remain faithful within the land. In the bigger picture, God's creation was a purposeful and peace-filled place for His people. From Eden to the Promised Land and ultimately to the eternal land, He promises this to the faithful. So for us today, this land is not a particular place, city, street, or occupation. Those things, of course, could be part of it, but *the land* we are called to is simply our life and our purpose in it. A faithful, joyful, and purpose-filled life where God has placed us at any given moment. Even if you are exactly where you want to be or still aspiring for answers, *your land* is simply living boldly and fearlessly for God's hand and will in all of it right where you are. Living in gratefulness for what God has done and anticipation of what is to come. *Your land* is where you want to be that is sanctioned and prepared by God, and your only desire is to be front and center in it. Claiming your land means that you have agreed with your Creator that you have an immensely important part in His kingdom, and you don't want to miss a minute of it. God has land set apart for us all. He has given us life and a way to live it to the fullest. Joshua claimed his. Now it is our turn.

Find this story in Joshua 1-8

PREPARING FOR THE LAND

The story of Joshua gives us directives that I think will help us tap into the bravery of the women of Luke more clearly when we apply God's intentions for all of His people behind them. Joshua's courage is remarkable and invigorating and makes me want to run to take on the world. His bravery came from one place: faith in God.

He never ever fancied the idea that God would not come through. He set his sights on what God told him was his and he took it. I mean physically and mentally took it. He knew that this was what he was created for and he was not about to miss it. He cleaned out and destroyed everything that God told him to. He let nothing get in his way of having land that had his name on it. He corrected the mistakes he let get by him. He never looked left or right or cared for a second what others were doing or what they may say about what he was doing. I want that type of faith. To turn from anything that is not God-approved or ordained for my life. To become that person, we have to look way beyond this tiny world and to the greater picture of God's vast kingdom and our part in accommodating that vastness. We must look past our little white picket fence world and into the lens of what we were created for outside of it. We have to get geared up to fight against the desires of this world and seek to walk spiritually alive, leading solely to all things eternal.

In the last chapters of Deuteronomy, Moses hands over the baton to Joshua, installing him as Israel's new leader and land-taker. He sings a song of remembrance lest they forget why they are standing at the edge of their promise. He re-instills the beneficiary acts of Abraham and reminds them they are the new generation that will take the promises to fruition. Moses does not leave out the failures of their forefathers and the losses they endured as a warning of the temptations that may lie ahead. He brings blessings to the tribes as he washes off the old in order to remind them of the new awaiting them. He leaves Joshua with five words that will be a strong reminder of his purpose moving forward: "These words are your life" (32:7). These words will be the basis for the prosperity and peace that God's wandering tribes have longed for. A place of unity and cohesiveness as a faithful people, where worship of the one true God of Israel would be consistent and unmovable and a starting point to becoming the beacon of hope for the rest of the world. These last chapters of reminder and instruction would serve as the foundation that could either make or break their future. Each word was meant to keep them focused on the straight and narrow path that would bring into being all that had been promised for centuries.

One of the first things Joshua did before setting foot into the new land was to *remember* what God had done for the nation of Israel. Remembering God's provision is a benefit to the soul. It washes away the negative vibes that carry us off to the wilderness. It straightens our spines, strengthens our hearts, and reminds us that we all were made to be Joshuas. There are many times in our life that things won't go our way. There are detours, distractions, and disappointments, not to mention some down-right darkness that can and will, at times, envelope us all. But when we remain focused on the deeds and character of God laid out for us in Old Testament history, and better yet, our own personal lives, we are strengthened in that moment. We can reset in that "aha" moment and move forward in the glory of the past. In Psalm 143:5, David, in his fear of Saul, who is chasing him to kill him, looks back over what God has done for strength in that moment. He says, "*I remember the days of old; I meditate on all that you have done; I ponder the work of your hands.*" He knows that to make it out alive and take the land that was his as the King of Israel, he would need everything God had given him. He repents, asks for mercy, and then remembers God's mighty acts and asks Him to do it again. Whether we are trapped in a bad situation or entering into unknown territory, knowing who God is and what He has done for all of creation and each of us, will empower us to fierce faith and obedience. Our past with God is the moving sidewalk into our future, and we should bring it with us wherever we go. Like Joshua, take it into your land and unpack it. Remember what God has done for you, and if He has called you to read this, you can be assured His faithfulness is real.

TAKING THE LAND

"Dress for success" is an old business saying that encourages us to show up like we already have what it is we came for. Dressed and ready to receive. Joshua was the epitome of it. His story begins with his immediate call by God to enter the land and *receive* what is already his. First, he says, *"I will give you every place where you set your foot"* (1:1-9). He sandwiches this with even more promises to never leave or forsake and to always be faithful to him. God has dressed Joshua for success and all it required was walking in and taking it. By starting with a foundation of remembrance and gratefulness, his launching pad was secure. He had all the confidence he needed to walk right into the promised land and receive all that was waiting there.

Before Joshua actually took the land, he had to move out the inhabitants that were there. These people were ungodly and immoral and could easily corrupt God's chosen people, distracting them from their faithful purpose. This would call for a physical fight to conquer this land. There are two battles that have to be fought upon entrance and these two stories are crystal clear in their direction. In the battles of Jericho and Ai, God promised that by listening and obeying His wartime instructions, these enemies would easily be defeated. In fact, He actually says, *"I have delivered Jericho into your hands."* I mean, it's done. God had already done the work. He just needed faithful warriors. Hands and feet on the ground to do the work on His behalf. Joshua in his steadfast obedience was the faithful warrior who brought victory and glory to God that day.

The Battle of Ai, not so much (Joshua 7). Greed entered, and God was not trusted for provision. Sin and disobedience entered and separated God's people. Lives were lost. It says in Joshua 7:5 that *the hearts of the people melted in fear and became like water.*" Lost strength, lost faith, drowning in fear and inability. Right off the bat, we get a very clear lesson about taking the land—obedience brings confidence and life; disobedience brings fear and death.

This loss in battle is a clear indicator of what sin in one person's life will do to the whole bunch. One bad apple. . .(Well, I think you get it). We are assured here that our sins will be found out, and not only will it disconnect us from God, but it will usurp the whole community. Sin festers, flows, and corrupts. People died in battle because of Achan's decision to look out for himself. His whole family was destroyed. This is a team playing at its worst. Although God's word is intimate and personal, it is meant for the community at large. So if you choose to sin, it will affect others, no matter how hard you try to hide it. How is that? For one, your shame and guilt will keep you from being all you are supposed to be. You will always be hiding a part of yourself and thus, a part of God, from those around you who might need to pull from your strength. You will miss your call and purpose for sure and waste a lot of valuable time. Your secret self will be a lie, therefore constantly keeping you at work trying to hide it. More energy will go to the things hidden than living out in the open, free to be fully yourself.

These two battles show us that victory only comes when we have our eyes on God. It's when we try to take matters into our own hands, try to control the situation, or work the system that failure is a sure thing. Joshua trusted God, listened and obeyed, and walked right out into victory. It was as simple as that. Nothing else to discuss or attempt. No dry runs or hopes for the best. They would be empowered by this win and unified as a nation. This victory would be the motivator to keep them pushing forward in the will of God.

Jesus is the reason we have the same ability and motivation to stay on a winning streak. He cleared the slate for us, and in our repentance and acceptance of His life and death by our faith, we too will be victorious in the battles of this world. No matter the size of the enemy, the number of weapons we might use, or even the scars we might walk away with, victory will always be ours because this battle called life belongs to God. He has called us, empowered us, and waits for our faithfulness so that He might bring about the victory He longs to give us.

When you decide to walk with God into battle, well, decide to walk with God. Let God destroy any sin, past and present, and anything that is hindering us from taking the land. Stand up to the enemy, and do not believe one lie he is spouting, because that is what he does. He will tell you that you are inept, prideful, wrong, and my personal favorite, *too old,* but those are all lies. The enemy loves to cast doubt and fear. He will speak your negative language right to your face, and you will want to agree with him because it is easier to sit back and do nothing than to be fierce and faithful and believe that Satan actually resides under your feet. In Numbers 13, Joshua and Caleb were the only two in the first attempt at taking the land that believed it could be done. Everyone else doubted and shrunk back, believing the status quo was easier than having to fight for what was already theirs. So there will still be those people; walk past them. God will send them back for another jaunt in the wilderness while you rest in your promised land.

STAYING IN THE LAND

The last thing Joshua shows us about taking our land is my absolute favorite. We can take the land victoriously, but we must also abide in it faithfully. Scripture doesn't tell us a lot about Joshua other than he is fearless, but I came across this one short sentence that I think sums up exactly who he is. In Exodus 33:1-11, God's people have reached Mt. Sinai on their journey to the Promised Land, and Moses and Joshua have set up the tent of meetings for people to come and go with inquiries to the LORD. Moses would enter to meet with God "face to face like a friend." But the very last sentence says, "*Joshua, son of Nun, never left the tent.*" This speaks of a dedicated and intentional man of God who is there for a purpose. It shows that Joshua was a devoted and humble servant way before he was a courageous leader. While Moses returned to camp, Joshua remained in the tent. He knew God would be back, with a word, an instruction, and he wasn't going to miss it. Joshua abided patiently and faithfully, awaiting God's presence, knowing that success would only come through Him.

Getting in is one thing, staying in is another. God instructed Joshua (1:8) to *"keep this Book of the Law, meditate on it day and night . . . so that you will be prosperous and successful."* Staying in the land is the goal, but success and purpose are the icing on the cake. Trusting that wherever God sends us, He will provide for us, and we will always land on our feet. We will never be left in lack but will have exactly what we need with enough to share. Remember, as His image-bearers we were created to manage, increase, and subdue, but it only comes from knowing God and trusting His Word. It is so easy to get lost in the land when we are looking in all directions. No doubt we are pulled in by many encouraging and instructive words from all types of spiritual people, and we need those in our lives. But when it comes to staying on the solid ground of life, our feet need to be anchored in the Word of God. You can go to church, hang out with Christians, and listen to great sermons, but until you begin to meditate, search, and research the Bible, you will never know who God is and what He has to say to you. The Bible is the story of God's people and you are one of them. He is talking to you and has much to say. Reading the Bible invites us into our own story. We are the "all" in the "all the generations" that Abraham was promised in Genesis 12:1-2. It did not end after the first century. It will continue until we are with Him in eternity. I purchased a study Bible when I first started to seek God that was filled with all types of notes, bios, and historical information. He helped me understand the author, his intent on writing, the history of this great world, and how they all were woven together. I also went to in-depth Bible studies where I was taught how to study purposefully. Now that doesn't mean that you have to go all academic on it, but just by simply picking it up and investing some time each day, along with a great devotional, you will definitely have all you need to stay (and be victorious) in your land.

Like Joshua, we must believe that wherever God calls us is ours for the taking. We own it. It has been waiting for us to arrive. We will be a success there. We can read this all day long, but when will we believe it and take it? Believe me, this journey is not an overnight success story. Ask Moses. You will fall, you will turn around, you will doubt, and Satan will mess with you like never before, but once you start heading toward your land, abiding in His presence, God will guide you all the way there. What is meant for God's people (that would be me and you) we already have. Remember, we have *everything*. All we need. But we have to participate to receive it. It is about agreeing with your Maker that you are part of something greater than your years here on earth. It is not about what you obtain, make, do, or accomplish unless it has God's kingdom stamp of approval on it. We must agree that we are part of a much greater plan than just simply existing and working hard to make sure our life is up to par with what the world demands. In fact, it is just the opposite. Taking on your new self will cost you your old self, and that is not an easy task, but it is doable with Jesus. God is faithful, and He will spin you and spin you until all those bolts are loosened and you are free to be entirely His.

REST IN THE LAND

Now, there is an amazing gift that goes with this land. It's called rest. Did I just hear you sigh? Like yes, rest, I want some of that. I think that word is at the top of every woman's list of needs. Yes, we do need rest from the multi-tasking events of our everyday lives and the chaos that awaits us early each morning. Beautiful as that chaos can be sometimes, it is still chaos. This particular rest that awaits the people of Israel runs much deeper, becoming the very foundation from which all the mundane things of life flow. God promises not just land but rest inside that land. In fact, He identifies the land as the rest itself when God instructs Joshua that He will "give you rest by giving you this land." So, in other words, the land is the beautifully wrapped package, and the rest is the gift inside. It's already there and it's waiting to be opened.

We can now understand that by listening to our own thoughts and emotions, enlisting our own desires and talents, and seeking the Lord's purpose and plan for our lives, we have entered into a new territory where we can rest in all things God. I mean really rest in Him. We might still wonder, maybe question a thing or two, but we have learned not to act on those things but to wait on Him by abiding in our tent. We are now attached to His greater good, and there is no way we are letting go. Things are clearer, the world has moved out from under us a little, and we have our eyes on a much grander prize. Wow, rest. I like it here.

TIME OF REFLECTION

- Am I willing to let God do anything in me or through me that has been made possible through the atonement of the Cross of Christ?
- What course of action can I take that will begin to exhibit Christ in me?
- Where can I begin to show obedient faith in God in a specific area of my life?
- What land (thing, place, position, ministry, person) has God placed before me that I need to move toward conquering?
- What is keeping me from going? Who/What is standing in my way?
- What are the what-ifs or fears that keep me from stepping out in fierce faith?
- What/Who do I need to clear out of my land so that I can be prosperous and successful?
- What battle am I trying to win on my own? What do I need to trust God with completely?

SCRIPTURAL PRAYER: *Praise be to the LORD my Rock, who trains my hands for war, my fingers for battle. He is my loving God and my fortress, my stronghold, my deliverer, my shield, in whom I take refuge, who subdues people under me. (Psalm 144)*

PERSONAL PRAYER: *Thank you, Father for showing me who you are and all that you have done for me. Like the men and women of old may I be brave enough to take the steps that you are calling me to. Give me the willingness to obey and the perseverance to continue as I humbly and lovingly seek to do your will. Help me to look at obstacles straight on knowing and trusting that you will overcome all things that keep me from serving you. Guide me onto your path, Lord, and keep me ever close to you. Amen.*

CHAPTER FOUR

THE GOSPEL TRUTH

❧

MATTHEW, MARK, LUKE, and John are the four gospels of the New Testament that establish the foundation of Jesus' mission seen through His life, death, and resurrection. These four narratives share this *"good news"* through the eyes of Spirit-ordained authors whose stories are delivered through their own unique qualities and personal touch. Matthew, Mark, and Luke are referred to as the *synoptic* gospels because they share many common features while describing Jesus' life and ministry to their differing audiences.

On the other hand, John's coverage of this narrative is unique in its deliverance as well as an addition of stories and events not found in the previous gospels. Although they all vary in some way, the final story comes together with no missing pieces. The truth that continually flows through is that Jesus Christ is the Messiah, the Suffering Servant, the Savior for all, and the Son of God. For the purposes of this study, we will focus on the gospel of Luke and his inclusivity of the faithful women who were prominent in Jesus' life.

THE AUTHOR

Unlike the other gospels who wrote to vast groups, Luke writes to a singular recipient, the most "excellent" Theophilus, with the purpose of reassuring him of the "certainty of the things you have been taught"(1:3). This leads one to believe that Theophilus, a gentile, was just discovering the Old Testament history of the nation of Israel that began with Abraham, and now Luke is systematically walking him through the completion of God's salvific plan found in Jesus Christ. It can only be hoped that through this one man's possible interest in Israel's history and promising future, his account will be spread among his contemporaries and is the true purpose for Luke's comprehensive coverage of the life and ministry of Jesus.

Paul's reference to his friend, Luke, as "the doctor" in

his farewell letter to the Colossians (4:14) also helps bring a clearer picture of the "orderly account" referenced in Luke's gospel introduction. This intellect could possibly reflect his thoroughness in his investigation and research that differs from the other gospels. Luke's involvement with Paul's travels, eyewitness and oral accounts, as well as employment of historical facts, round out his unique perspective of God's covenant fulfillment in Jesus. Luke's authorship of the book of Acts, a sequel to his gospel and written to Theophilus as well, connects Christ's ministry to the works of the church and helps us better understand how the Gospels correspond to Paul's letters and epistles of the New Testament. In Luke's second letter, he continues to confirm to his singular recipient that the outward growth of the church community along with its struggles and persecution is a direct result of God's plan, through Jesus, to move this good news throughout the world. His point is to override any thought that God's mission would be an easy one. There would be no military coup or mountaintop advancement for his people. God's movement through Jesus to the faithful would be a spiritual battle that would only be won by fighting the good fight, trusting only in their Savior for the victory.

My affinity for Luke is not simply his promotion of the women that headline his narrative. First and foremost, I believe Luke's historical foundation is one that tells us that yes, faith in the life and purpose of Jesus as our Savior is imperative, but knowing and understanding our Creator God and His full purpose for sending His Son is important to building a deep foundation of faith. The Old Testament timeline of God's story, which Luke works to unfold, brings to life the people, places, and culture that reveal who God is from creation to re-creation of His people through Abraham. To know God at His fullest, we must seek to find Him in these beginning stories.

HIS HUMANITY

Beginning not just with Jesus' birth but reaching back to the birth of John the Baptist shows Luke's desire to preserve the full history of God's plan for creation. He steps back into prophesy's fulfillment of John the Baptist (Isaiah 40:3-5) to cement Jesus' arrival into the world. He works to leave no room for gaps or inaccuracies that might lead one off course in their personal journey to faith. He makes history personal with family and close relatives, which makes Jesus' arrival simple and easily identifiable. Luke continues to prove the man Jesus through His genealogical roots found in Luke 3 that begin, not with Abraham as the gospel of Matthew traces, but through the line of Joseph as the earthly father that brought Him into being. Luke invites us to walk among His people. Common everyday people, doing common everyday things as God does the miraculous amongst them. Luke's birth stories are exciting and are meant to make us feel welcome to walk along with them. Luke's detailed recounting of Jesus' short life and ministry is an invitation to see for ourselves this wonderful event and to walk carefully toward our own reception of God's Son who was sent as the Savior to the world. Luke writes to show all people, Jew and Gentile alike, that as believers it is up to us to seek to discover these facts and the meanings in these historical accounts of Jesus' human and divine mission and our place in this life-changing story.

Both of these birth stories are written in a way that is easy to relate to and draw us in faith as we put Jesus' life together piece by piece. This is to help us come to full confidence in God's saving plan for His people, how it began, and where it will lead. In contrast to Mark, Matthew, and John's gospels that move quickly into Jesus' ministry, death, and resurrection, Luke begins by showing us the man Jesus. The humanness of family and boyhood and ultimately His prophesied announcement by John the Baptist who readies the world for its new king. Through these details, we realize quickly that Jesus did not show up accidentally or on His own. He was promised in detail, planned on by many, and His way prepared. History has been waiting on this day, and Luke makes sure the foundation is secure as he shows us who Jesus was, is, and is to come.

HIS DIVINITY

Luke's initial purpose is shown in the perfect humanity of Jesus that will ultimately reveal God's divine nature existing wholly within Him. His humanity secures His relatability, but it is His divine nature that will reset the course of the world. Even amid the commonness of His birth, the supernatural is flourishing as we realize that this family was handpicked by God to bring about His purpose and plan. Their realization of their own ineptness and yet humbled by God's desire to use them is the beginning example of the attitude required to walk among them as God's chosen. Luke continues to reveal who Jesus is through His victory over Satan in the wilderness, proving His perfect nature and setting His perfection apart from all humanity.

Luke quickly reveals God's saving plan through Jesus' miracles that heal the sick and bring the dead to life. Although the Gospels of Matthew and Mark share many of the same miraculous accounts as Luke, the latter holds the distinction of being the "Savior" to the least and the lost. In fact, in Luke 19:9, Jesus refers to Himself as the "*Son of Man* who has come to seek and save those who are lost." Not the greatest, richest, most educated. Not those who have performed, achieved, and are enough in this world. The people in Luke's gospel are emphasized by their lack and need. Those who have failed and those who are lost and hopeless. Outcasts, dropouts, shadows on the backdrop of life's successes. The example Luke uses is not to tell us that we have to be down and out, destitute and diseased to receive Jesus, but rather, it is a visual of what our heart truly looks like without Him in it. Luke's portrayal of Jesus' compassion for the suffering of those of lesser societal class is used to show God's reversal of standards where humble submission replaces prideful position for entry into His kingdom and at the same time, using their earthly plight as a visual of the human need for a savior. Sitting on top of the world without the need of a Savior is, in Luke's eyes, destitution at its finest. Those who fell at the feet of Jesus, knowing their lack and trusting He was the one to fill the void, were the success stories in his narrative. They didn't come to Jesus seeking wealth and riches, comfort and joy. They sought healing and fulfillment at the deepest level that only came from the touch of their Savior's hand.

Luke's purpose is to show God's mission through Jesus as one that brings a reversal to societal norms by moving the least and the lost to the head of the line. Through the brokenness of society's lesser-thans, Luke shows Jesus' arrival as one of compassion and restoration that will bring God's lost people back into His created order. Luke's account sets out to prove God's purpose in sending Jesus as the one true Savior in contrast to the modern-day rulers who deem themselves worthy of this title.

These stories work to show the fruition of the history of God's chosen people, Israel, starting with the covenant of Abraham to the laws handed down to Moses, renewed by kings, and carried on by faithful prophets. Luke's writing is purposeful and not to just tell the story again but to systemically acknowledge where the past meets the present and God's divine hand in it all. He works to pull Israel out of their present-day circumstances that drive them to fantasize about this promised Messiah who will usurp the cruel dictatorship of Roman rule and set them up as God's elected people and who will physically rule above all others. They took their call as "a great nation" as a literal one, a worldly position stopping short of its divine nature.

Luke's gospel shows that God's kingdom to come has arrived. No longer is there a need to wait. The Messiah is here and He has brought all they will ever need. They now must acknowledge that yes, Rome may still rule their circumstances, but God is ruler of their hearts. God's glory is evident in their faithfulness, and their greatness comes only from their servanthood. Luke shows that the Messiah's arrival is not to give Israel an edge over others but to lead others out of the wilderness. God's chosen people will now fulfill their purpose as beacons shining a light on the Savior the world has been promised.

The bigger picture found in Luke's account is that God's salvific plan for Israel will also continue into the hearts of the Gentiles and the world altogether. This plan has been put into motion by God and will only happen through God. Luke draws for his reader a grand scope of the promised deliverance of the nation of Israel, brought to fruition through Jesus' arrival. He works to certify that what has been read, heard, and promised has now been fulfilled in Jesus Christ. Luke begins with Jesus as the Son of Man and ends with the announcement of Jesus as the Son of God. Luke connects the dots of Jesus' life and ministry up to His death and ascension, all to confirm His identification with humanity. His portrayal of Jesus as the perfect human leading to the perfect sacrifice that confirms Him as the world's Savior is the foundation of his writings that invite us into this divine family through faith in this amazing gift.

Read Isaiah 52:13 - 53:1-12

The resounding difference found in Luke's gospel is his surplus of feminine perspectives surrounding the life of Jesus. These various women are instrumental in showing Luke's view of God's true purpose and plan for the nation of Israel predominantly and the whole world ultimately. By using the example of the weak and oppressed in society, Luke offers the believer the same opportunity by showing them the pathway to righteousness that opens the door to the kingdom of God. Beginning with

His humble birth, Luke introduces Jesus through the eyes of Elizabeth and Mary. The fierce faith of these young mothers-to-be shows how God intervenes in the lives of the most unlikely and unqualified to bring His divine message into the world. Just as God restored Israel out of bondage and into a new land, Luke's short but miraculous stories include many women healed by Jesus' simple touch to prove the Father's love for the least. In a society where greatness and personal value were seen as the peak of success, Jesus turned the tables to show the opposite for which He came. Luke culminates his story with the women who, after coming face to face with Jesus, have chosen to follow Him with their lives. We find them walking along in His ministry, standing afar to mourn His death, and being the first on the scene of His resurrection.

Whether Luke was a doctor or not will always be open for debate, but his compassion for the well-being of God's broken people is evident in his portrayal of these women who stand out as Jesus' friends throughout His ministry on earth. Luke's gospel shows how the fierce faith of these women called by God, healed by His hand, and restored to a life that glorifies His name can only be realized through faith in Jesus Christ. Something that is readily available to us today.

TIME OF REFLECTION

- How has the study of the Gospel of Luke enlightened your understanding of Jesus' life and ministry?

- Write down three things that you didn't know about the Gospels before this study. How has this changed your belief or strengthened your faith?
- If you had to write a story of Jesus in your own life, what would it be about? What things has He done in your life, i.e. blessings, and suffering, that have strengthened your faith and proven who He is?
- How would you tell someone about the Gospel story? Practice with yourself or a friend. Write it down, along with your personal testimony, in your journal to go back to as needed.
- Have you ever testified to someone about what God has done?

SCRIPTURAL PRAYER: *For this reason I kneel before the Father, from whom every family in heaven and on earth derives its name. I pray that out of his glorious riches he may strengthen you with power through his Spirit in your inner being, so that Christ may dwell in your hearts through faith. And I pray that you, being rooted and established in love, may have power, together with all the Lord's holy people, to grasp how wide and long and high and deep is the love of Christ, and to know this love that surpasses knowledge—that you may be filled to the measure of all the fullness of God. Now to him who is able to do immeasurably more than all we ask or imagine, according to his power that is at work within us, to him be glory in the church and in Christ Jesus throughout all generations, forever and ever. (Ephesians 3:14-21)*

PERSONAL PRAYER: *Father God, I pray for discernment and understanding in my study of Your Word. Help me know You as my Savior, who came to save me from my sin. Guide me to others who know You deeply and to those who need You deeply. Send faithful friends who encourage me in my faith. People of depth and discernment who share their walk easily and openly. Who listen without judgment. Who build up with every word. Help those seeking to open their minds to the new and release the old. Leaving the past behind to walk nearer to Your kingdom plans. Spill over in their hearts so that Your love will come full circle. Through them and out into the world. May Your Word come alive with purpose and meaning.*

CHAPTER FIVE

FIERCE FAITH BEGINS

൭

THE BOOK OF Luke begins with the story of birth. Birth is a powerful foundation for women. Not that you have to give birth to be a powerful and brave woman, but to know that God has given this special ability only to women lays the foundation of our fierceness. The divinely orchestrated birth story of Elizabeth and Mary will not only stimulate the desire set into God's re-creation purposes but drive us to keenly focus on our own fierce call. So we are going to start with the birth of Jesus because birth just shouts a new beginning, and then you have Jesus, so I mean, what's better than that?

In the first chapter of Luke, we read about Zechariah and Elizabeth, descendants of Aaron and part of the priestly tribe. The story tells us that they are "righteous in the sight of God; blameless and obedient even." The "in the sight of God" statement is key because it means that this was not only a community opinion of their spiritual maturity but one where God reigned in their lives. They worked hard to remain faithful to all the laws and commands and especially their temple duties to stay on the good side of God. Even in all of this, they still found themselves without because of their inability to conceive a child. But that will all change when an angel comes face to face with Zechariah and promises their suffering will soon end. The key point of this story is not only God's amazing arrival in the midst of their heartfelt need but the divine anointing He brings over this family. Even in spite of Zechariah's doubtful response, God's mission to fulfill His promise of a Messiah is on a direct course, and Zechariah and Elizabeth are key players in His mission.

As we enter into the story of Jesus' birth, all is well with Elizabeth as she is six months pregnant with John the Baptist, and Mary, after hearing her own good news, comes to visit her cousin. Now, of course, Mary's story is incredible and the purpose of well, everything, but we have to give Elizabeth some credit here as well. Her voice is heard as the one that confirms Mary's divine call and position. We all need that person whom we can confide in, share our fears and joys with, and whose fetus jumps for joy when ours enters the room. Am I right? Elizabeth's pregnancy is two-fold in that it introduces John the Baptist as the one prophesied by Isaiah (40:3-5) to introduce our Savior to the world in God's perfect time as well as to cement Mary's call. The story of these two women begins with Elizabeth's first words that will answer any and every question swirling through Mary's head. Before Mary can whimper a sound upon her arrival, her Spirit-filled cousin blesses her as the *mother of our Lord.*" Elizabeth poured wisdom and encouragement over her cousin-friend and left no room for doubt or fear, paving the way for Mary's fierceness to surface. The story does not tell us what Mary was feeling exactly, but we do know that when these two women met, their Spirit-filled energy moved Elizabeth to become the tangible answer that would establish Mary as the mother of all mothers.

Elizabeth's fierceness grew out of suffering. She was barren in a society that left her with guilt over this physical incapability. Children were a gift. A blessing. So if you weren't able to conceive, then the problem falls on you. I mean, the word *barren* does not have an especially nice ring to it to begin with. This is proven in Genesis 16 when Sarah's desperate plight with infertility led her to desperate measures. She went out of God's will to procure a child for herself through Hagar, and one can only believe that the judging eyes around her might have sent her on that path. But in this story, Elizabeth's humbleness from this blessing is felt as she embraces Mary and brings forth a heartfelt celebration of God's hand in her life. It is all good in Elizabeth's world. She has seen the Lord's faithfulness in a seemingly impossible way and consequently, her fierceness was contagious. Two unassuming women, one might say, the least of these, miraculously united to physically bring good news to the world.

Let me just interrupt to express that as one who was infertile, I feel honored to be in association with the likes of Elizabeth (as well as Sarah and Hannah), so if you are out there in the midst of this trial, hang on. God is carrying you in His right hand, and there is a grand purpose in it all. This is not a place for the faint of heart. God has allowed something that He knows for sure you can handle, so hang on girlfriend. You've got this. God will use it to the heights to glorify Himself and to bless you abundantly in one way or another. Rest in that land for a minute. No slight to my sweet fertile friend who had four kids while I waited for one, but honestly, when my daughter was born, I felt she was basically ordained and ready for her crown. There never was and never will there be anything more special than the birth of a long-awaited, blubbered-over, stomped-my-feet-for child! God is good. He not only gives life and blessing, but He will also turn you into an "Elizabeth" who will give hope and encouragement that enables you to pay it forward. I have no doubt that Mary's fear was tempered and her fierceness enhanced by the love and joy expressed toward her by the humbled and grateful spirit of her cousin-friend. Elizabeth had seen a mighty God do a mighty thing, and she was certain He was about to do it again.

As we know, prophecy is found throughout the Old Testament regarding the coming of a savior, but we also can be assured of this divine union of births by Isaiah's prophecy of "a voice of one calling in the wilderness...," namely John the Baptist. All this to say, no coincidences here. There is divine power in this story and by no means a fluke surrounding the timely conception of these two historical men. The narrative of Jesus' short but earth-shattering life backed up by preachers, teachers, theologians, and thousands of years of changed lives around the world can also be traced back throughout historical chronicles. Not to mention archaeology in and around most of the biblical lands that dredge up ancient logs, writings, and diagrams that continually prove our faith on a regular basis. My point here is that what the Bible tells us was happening around Jesus as He walked this earth, well, was really happening. This is no fairy tale with made-up narratives to give us great sound bites. It gives even greater power to God's word to know that it was not some far-off distant land that no one had heard about. It was real life in a real place, that Jesus walked right into, well, He was born into...He walked a little later.

What I want is for you to grasp the divineness and

realness of this story so that we can walk together along-side these two fierce women who gave this story breath and fully understand where they are coming from. We not only admire them and rejoice with them, but we can relate to their woman-ness as we long for that same fierceness to come alive in our own lives. Before we enter into the sanctuary of Mary's heart, let us first uncover the life in which she lived and what this event looked like to the outside world of that day. Based on the timeline of Jesus' birth, history gives us a very good indicator of the Roman culture in which the nation of Israel existed. Not only can we find out about their home life, culture, religion, and entertainment, but in particular the daily life of a woman. So we can put ourselves in this place as a woman and especially as a woman giving birth to the Savior of the world.

Could you imagine living in the first century, unmar-ried and pregnant? There is a lot to this story. A lot of supernatural divine-ness, God-moving intervention that keeps us from having to worry a bit about its outcome, but realistically, let us not forget that real life is real life, and Mary had to deal with a good bit of it before this all worked out. So to say she is fierce doesn't do it justice. I am not saying that Mary did not have a moment or two of anxiety. She is human after all. But that is not record-ed here. What is recorded is her immediate departure to see Elizabeth. That is where any fear was replaced by the confirmation by her dear cousin of what was happening in her life. All brought about by the Holy Spirit to give Mary clarity and peace so that no time would be wasted on worldly influence that would only discourage her. As the Spirit confirmed her through Elizabeth, she sang a song praising God for His calling on her life, showing her humble faith in the One she trusts with her whole being. How in the world can she sing praise to God before she even fully understands the dire consequences that await or the possibilities of all the "what ifs?" The answer lies in one single, solitary sentence in Luke 1:35 when Elizabeth exclaims, *"Blessed is she who has believed that the Lord would fulfill his promises to her."* Bingo. She believed that God would do what He said He would do.

Let's compare her faith to Zechariah's response. I think it lends to us the benefit of understanding working in faith and waiting in humility. Zechariah (Elizabeth) and Mary were given the same promise—the birth of a child—two unlikely candidates I might add. In God's quest for the faithful, their responses to the call help us see the difference and ultimately define the origins of fierce faith. Zechariah was no doubt a religious man and godly leader, and I am sure he learned a great lesson on that day the angel greeted him. He questions the likelihood of *if* this will happen and loses the opportunity of a lifetime. As a priest, this was the day he longed for. To be called by God. He knew the stories of Abraham, Moses, Samuel, and the many prophets who had experienced the voice of God. What priest would not most likely long for that moment? Zechariah missed it and lost his voice in the process. Let's not forget that God's plan was not thwarted or interrupted in the least by Zechariah's doubt. The only one who lost that day was Zechariah. He missed out on being a part of an amazing event. He was there but not completely. Let that be an example to us all. When God calls...just say yes.

In contrast, Mary received the angel's pronouncement. Not doubting but only seeking to know *"how."* Mary is a virgin, so the devil is in the details here (no pun intended). Any attempts on how this would take place are lost on her, so knowing exactly how this was going to happen was important, not about if. No uncertainty, just maybe a simple roadmap. She did not protect herself like Abraham, offer excuses like Moses, or wrestle like Jacob. And in contrast to Zechariah, she did not lose her voice. Instead, she sang a song. A song of praise for the blessing that had been given her. Mary's song of praise called, *"the Magnificat,"* found in Luke 1, reveals her delight at being called to magnify God as His humble servant. Even in light of the cultural standards that would likely be held against her, she said yes, immediately. Mary's mental and emotional acceptance of her calling brought about a fulfillment for the entire nation of Israel. Her response put into motion the corrective measure needed to restore humanity from that fateful day in the garden. A new matriarch that would bring forth hope for mankind. Her yes was a finality of centuries of wilderness walking for God's people. The sin of the world would lose its grip on God's creation. This child, her child, Jesus, would once and for all unite mankind back to the Father as intended in the beginning. Mary had the whole world in her hands, and she gratefully received it for our sake. Now we can put to rest any questions about Eve's indiscretions and replace them with the fierce obedience of this brave woman and mother-to-be. The foundation is laid; everything to see is here. Women, we were made for this type of fierceness. Founded on the power of birth that we alone possess to pay the way forward by multiplying and increasing God's earth with new lives of faith. This is our humble servitude to a God who gives strength to women like none other.

God used a woman to bring about our true re-creation through the incarnation of Jesus. Frightened and as fragile as she might have seemed, she quickly turned into the woman God called her to be. A force of fierce. In Genesis 2, God created woman with her own uniqueness as a helper to man in God's great kingdom plan. United in their efforts, the individual roles of man and woman are expanded on throughout scripture and reveal an assignment to be accomplished together. There is no power struggle here. Each role complements the other in respect, humility, and responsibility. These scriptures reveal that women have an important and satisfying part in God's divine universal plan, and we should never lose sight of it. There is a place of participation for women in every factor of the community of believers, and we have special talents, abilities, and gifts to prove it. But it is always alongside our brothers and sisters in Christ to help and encourage those inside and to bring about change for those on the outside. To define Paul's description of the children of God in Galatians 3:28, N. T. Wright writes, "The ground is even at the foot of the cross." So never forget who you belong to and most importantly, that as women we are not above any man and vice versa, but we deserve all the open doors presented before us. We are in this game together and, at this point, we are all helpers to one another, both deserving of love and respect.

The power of birth alone given to the woman in all its pain and harshness is something that we need to lay as the foundation of our fierceness. I think we can all agree that birthing a child is going to be painful and not to be seen as a type of punishment handed down because of garden indiscretions. I don't think there was ever any chance that giving birth would be easy. But instead, let us see this gift as the beautiful creation-increasing measure that it is. This gift given to women has certified us as co-creators for God's kingdom. Once again, continuing what He began and giving us power through the Spirit to do the same. So let's move forward with our focus on this ability *to go forth and multiply* as the one main ingredient that shows how much promise God has for us.

Sojourner Truth, a 19th-century African-American abolitionist and women's rights advocate, defended her position against those who say because Christ was a man, women are not equal. In her "Ain't I A Woman" speech, she eagerly responds by stating, *"Where did your Christ come from? From God and a woman! Man had nothing to do with Him."* To say the least, she took her role seriously and was not stepping aside for someone else's ancient opinions. She was the power that knocked down walls so that the rest of us could have the chance to speak up and out. Although her words might sound a tad harsh, even crude, and not meant to undermine the glory, goodness, and necessity of our man-people, here the truth lies. These words serve to encourage us in our fierce God-given abilities so that we might know and receive the unabashed acceptance of who we are in God's great kingdom, and like Sojourner, fear will have no place in our expression of who God created us to be.

Mary took this challenge of giving birth to our Savior with a grateful heart and gracefully walked into it with the conviction of a saint. She did not contemplate what was ahead of her. She didn't ponder the possibility that she would be ridiculed or ostracized from the community, that her betrothed would consider leaving her, that her child would renounce the safety of His family for His obedience to His true Father, that He would be tortured and would die a criminal's death for all to see. But her song of praise tells us what she did know: God had put a new song in her heart, and her son would be the final stanza.

Read these additional songs of praise in Luke 1:67-79, 2:12-14, 2:29-32

TIME OF REFLECTION

- Think about a time God divinely intervened in your life. Think about what God was revealing about Himself. About you?
- What storms/suffering has God allowed in your life? How have you grown spiritually from them? How have you responded/reacted to suffering in your life? Doubt? Faith? What did you learn?
- What are you hoping, dreading, fearing in your life? How are you letting Jesus lead the way?
- If someone described you spiritually, what adjectives would they use?
- Do you have an Elizabeth in your life? Someone who confirms what God is doing in your life? Someone who knows your gifts and calling?
- How can you testify to Him in your day-to-day life? In your attitude, gifts, or calling?

SCRIPTURAL PRAYER: *And Mary said, "My soul glorifies the Lord, and my spirit rejoices in God, my Savior, for he has been mindful of the humble state of his servant. From now on all generations will call me blessed; for the Mighty One has done great things for me, and holy is his name. His mercy extends to those who fear him, from generation to generation. He has performed mighty deeds with his arm; he has scattered those who are proud in their inmost thoughts. He has brought down rulers from their thrones but has lifted up the humble. He has filled the hungry with good things but has sent the rich away empty. He has helped his servant Israel, remembering to be merciful to Abraham and his descendants forever, just as he promised our ancestors." (Mary's Magnificat, Luke 1:46-55)*

PERSONAL PRAYER: *Heavenly Father, guide me as I walk in the shoes of the Marys of this world. Help me to be quick to obey my call to increase and multiply. Let me be fearless in my actions as I seek to follow their steps that lead to humble service to You. Thank You for empowering me with the ability to add unto Your kingdom, and help me to always sing a song of praise for all that You have done for me and for those that came before and those that will take the lead. Never let me forget the power You have given me and all women to bring new life in hopes of glorifying You more and more. Thank You, Father, for all my blessings, and give me the courage to persevere wherever You lead.*

CHAPTER SIX

FIERCE FAITH ENHANCED

※

I T HAS TAKEN me months to come to the place where I feel even remotely worthy to write my first word regarding healing. I have convinced myself that I must obtain some level of personal perfection in order to deliver any instruction regarding it. I have spent many hours writing it in my head, but when I sit before the keyboard, it is a blank slate. I actually offered to teach this book chapter by chapter to a few young women in my neighborhood in hopes that this healing chapter would catch up with me by the time I arrived at it. It didn't. I was, again, blank and actually worse than where I started. So I set it aside, feeling unhealed, unprepared, and unqualified to even write the alphabet. My frustration and lack of purpose stung. Now, many months later, I have realized that healing and wholeness are not something for me to laud over you but to walk alongside you. I think I was waiting for some big "a-ha" moment that would fill me with amazing wisdom and words that would fulfill and complete you (and me), only coming to the realization and acceptance of the fact that I am healed. I am whole. I have *everything* I need to tell you what I need to tell you, regardless of how joyful today is or what sorrows tomorrow brings. Yes, I have suffered and celebrated. I have been blessed and completely without. I have laughed, and I have cried. I have felt certain, and I have questioned it all. But what I know now is that my life does not need to be a symbol of perfection in order to guide you onto the road of healing and restoration. My healing story is not about my own personal struggles and experiences but is woven among the gospel stories that tell of Jesus' mission to redeem God's people through His death and resurrection. Any other details are only the journey to sanctification. Because of faith in Jesus, my healing is complete. In fact, the journey, good and bad, is what helps me guide you to the same place, and for that, I am so thankful. We were healed on the day of the cross, and our faith, hinged on God's mercy, is what moves us closer to the day of true perfection and holiness. Hope is what keeps us upright on the way.

When we talk about healing, our thoughts first go to the physical. We think of those suffering from physical ailments, disease, and pain. If not ourselves, those whom we love. In the gospels, we see miraculous physical healings. Although we know that He is entirely capable of this, we can all attest to the fact that He sometimes doesn't. It is a quandary that we find ourselves in as faithful believers as well as one that we have to leave at the altar of His mysteries. We don't understand why someone is not physically healed on the earthly side and we won't until we sit with Him in the new world, and probably by then it will be one less worry. But for now, we can attest to the fact that His healing as a spiritual one to those willing is one hundred percent.

Luke writes to show Jesus' arrival as the One who came for the lost and the least. Those who couldn't fight for themselves and whose life was often seen from the bottom of the barrel reaching up for a small ray of light. An upward fight for a simple taste of common ground. The outcast, the leper, the poor, the widowed, the abandoned, the orphaned, the enslaved, the oppressed, and in particular, the woman. Luke shares the plight of the woman in this ancient culture to reinforce Jesus' purpose of restoration and wholeness to those seen as anything but. Luke's Jesus came to heal all of humanity, and even though we might look compassionately into the lives of these ancient lesser-thans, what we have to realize is that we have all walked in their shoes. Luke uses the plight of the destitute to reveal His creation's need for salvation. All of Jesus' miraculous healings are meant to reveal to us that since the Fall of man, we were all lost and in need. Destitute in our sin. God's provision of the law for the nation of Israel was only a "guardian," Paul writes in Galatians 3:24, keeping them safe in His grace until Christ came. The law did not make them righteous or wipe away their sin, but Jesus as the perfect sacrifice would, and He did. Although these physical healings restored many back to their lives and families, the underlying and powerful message is that once they were touched by Jesus, they walked away with much more.

Jesus' mission led Him from town to town reaching out to those in need, touching, washing, and restoring the hopeless ones living in the belly of Israel's society. He not only touches them but moves them to rise up and accept their own healing. Oh, how I love a happy ending to a tragic story, but these stories are only the beginning. Through these interactions, Jesus is not just trying to get someone on their feet again, but rather, He has come to bring meaning and mission to their life, and not just to this life, but to invite them to an everlasting life to come. He is showing them the way to not only physical healing but calls them to accept this heavenly restoration that will bring them eternal healing and more, glory to God. This is a much bigger picture than someone being released from pain, inability, or even poverty. This is Luke showing us that God loved us so much that He gave up Jesus to restore us fully to Himself to never lack again. Jesus' restoration and healing of the lesser was meant to be an example of the greater. Much like the plagues brought about by Moses (Exodus 4) to unleash the Pharaoh's hold on an enslaved Israel, these mighty acts weren't simply for personal freedoms but to show God's desire for their full divine liberation of all and restoration of fellowship with Him. This is the bigger window we are looking into here. The outward healing is a gift, the inward is a necessity.

Regardless of our place or position in this life, our restoration has come, and we are able to live in it now. We have been healed by the Son. We are free from captivity to sin. We are actually given the freedom to choose not to sin. We have power over our own minds and bodies. Isaiah 61 prophesied that Jesus would take up our infirmities and bear our diseases. He took it and bore it on the cross to heal us from our sins and ourselves. He touched us. All so that we might be what God created us to be. He rebuked and drove it all out. We are restored, renewed, capable, and able. We have been resurrected with Him. We have crawled out of the darkness and are walking straight into the light of His presence. We can now walk in fellowship with our Creator God. We are fully and completely remade and rebuilt without lack. We now truly have *everything!* This is what is neatly entwined in every New Testament healing story. This is about spiritual salvation. These people were not just restored; they were made new. They walked away with more than they physically showed up with. They had seen Jesus face to face, and they would take Him with them wherever they went. Their healing, physical and spiritual, was a testimonial wildfire that would set the world aflame.

Out of the many miraculous stories, including Simon Peter's ailing mother-in-law, the woman with the crooked spine, and the death of the 12-year-old girl, the bleeding woman stands out to me over all others and really is what has driven me to write this book. It all began with an assignment in my late-in-life college adventure that led me to the women of Luke and to her in particular. Even when I questioned the sanity of the purpose of writing a book, I always thought of her. I think her story is imperative to the understanding of our spiritual healing. I have tried to lay a foundation that would lead to her and an understanding of what Jesus came to do. All the things I have discussed before, Elizabeth, Mary, Israel, and Joshua, were bringing us to her. She is the driving force that I want you to hold onto because she, too, walks with the label of *fierce*. This woman's life is relatable. She carries the torch for any and all who have had their life drained from them. All who have felt empty and weak. All that felt they were missing out on life and purpose or were oppressed, whether it be physically, mentally, or emotionally. All that have tried everything and walked away rejected and worse for wear. The fact that she doesn't have a name other than the bleeding woman tells us she could be anybody and yet she is everybody. Albeit her situation resonates with females in particular, it is her path to Jesus that helps us all see ourselves more clearly. It is at her feet that we should all sit to understand what it means to seek out Jesus and to be fully healed by His restorative touch.

This very short story begins in Luke 8:43-48. We are only given a few lines about her situation and her path to freedom. But it is powerful and one we must pay close attention to. Her story is also found in the gospels of Matthew and Mark and lends to Luke to help us see the fuller picture. To know this woman is to understand her daily life and culture. It is the first century. The #Me-Too movement is not an option. Women have no rights, no voice. They belong to their father and mother and then to their husbands. If they are lucky. If they never marry, they are pitied and usually become someone's servant. If they are widowed, they may become a ward of the temple, as Luke 18 shows us in the parable of the persistent widow. They did not receive rightful justice when it came to property and finances. They themselves could become property. Now this doesn't mean that they lived horrible and abusive lives. They had a purpose and a place. They were loved and respected by family and friends. It was just how it was. It is ancient history and freedoms weren't even the smallest of dreams because culture had yet to make room. Now let's talk about the bleeding woman. For this, we need to go back into the Old Testament and find out what "uncleanliness" meant to God's people and the responsibilities each had to not defile or be defiled.

When Moses rescued Israel from Egyptian slavery, he basically was given the task of training them in life skills. Beginning at Mt. Sinai, they are reunited with YHWH, the God of Israel, who begins to give a foundational shape to their life and community. Beginning with the law, which both covers their faithful relationship to Him as the one true God and their relationship with one another. They were also instructed on worship and ritual behaviors as well as temple-building instructions. In Leviticus 11-16, we get into the details of how sacrifices and temple worship were to be handled and maintained in order to guide and keep God's people set apart in faithfulness. First, uncleanliness was a thing. Whether it is coming from you or it came on you from someone else, it would automatically ostracize you from the community. Under the Old Testament Law, purity is a sign of holiness and that is God's mission for His people. Following these social and religious rules kept them in step with what God was calling them to be. These were outward signs that would set God's people apart from other nations and would allow Israel to show their obedience, love, and faithfulness back to the one true God.

Read Leviticus 12, 15, 18, 20

Purity in this ancient worship was meant as a sign of bringing their best selves before God in step with the lamb offered up during temple sacrificial service. There were certain foods, social practices, and physical attributes that had to be subdued in order to rightfully honor God in the Tabernacle and in life. In particular, female reproductive issues and any type of bodily emissions were two of the offenses that would keep you from worshiping or having fellowship within the community. Needless to say, the bleeding woman was suffering from something more than common feminine issues. She was actually hemorrhaging from somewhere in her body. This was serious and unstoppable from all accounts. According to the Gospel of Mark, she had seen many doctors who took her money and offered nothing back, especially healing. Even making it worse somehow, physically and most likely, mentally.

In Hebrew culture and worship, a woman in this situation wasn't allowed to socialize or touch objects for fear of contamination based on the rules of the Torah. She could return to normal life seven days after the natural bleeding had started and after she had lived separately from her family (Lev. 15.19). Unfortunately, the bleeding woman wasn't getting that break. For. Twelve. Years. Temple entrance and participation, as well as any festivals of atonement or celebration, were forbidden, leaving her spiritually deprived. She would have to be separated from her family during that time and if married, she had to live separately from her husband either in a room or a home without sexual relations and could even give her husband grounds to divorce her. Leaving her emotionally deprived as well. She couldn't go into the market or meeting areas where people gathered. She couldn't sit on a bench or touch objects that were common to others for fear of defiling them. It was something short of leprosy. I can only imagine how often she lived, counting off seven days, with her hopes dashed every time.

But in this story, we can deem a much deeper problem than just physical and emotional. Her story gives us a peak into God's restorative acts to those losing their life one day at a time. As sinners, that is exactly what was happening. Daily going through the motions, hoping to reach the day of atonement. Life becomes a wasteland of our attempts at cleanliness, of trying to be righteous and holy. Of the ball being dropped on a regular basis because we can never meet, on our own, the standards of a holy God. But as we see through this woman's experience, Jesus is the answer. He intervened in her loss and washed it all off of her. His power, not hers, entered and over-rode her efforts to cleanliness. Her life was healed and her loss was restored. This is the inward healing that God sent Jesus to do in and for all of us.

The blood is symbolic of life and death in the Bible. Jesus shedding His blood for us is significant to our salvation and new life. Through Jesus' blood, and His loss of life, we were redeemed, justified, and forgiven. The blood of the perfect Lamb is a powerful visual of His sacrifice for us. The loss of blood equals death. Blood in everyday terminology is a bodily fluid that sends necessary substances, i.e. much-needed nutrients and oxygen as well as taking out unwanted waste products. As Jesus proves, without the blood, there is no life. This woman was losing her blood; her life was slowly draining from her day by day. Can we all just moan for her for a minute? Can you imagine? Not only was she physically miserable, she was rejected by the community, the church, and even her family. She was unclean and untouchable. Emotionally and physically exiled. She was dead in her own life. I think it is clear that she was suffering. Horrendous, shameful, painful, embarrassing suffering. But her suffering is what brought her face-to-face with Jesus. She had come to the understanding that no one could do for her what she truly needed. Healing. Wholeness.

She wanted, one must believe, to be confident in herself. To walk with her head high. Restored to society and to her own life. To walk freely on this earth without fear and frustration. She needed to be saved from the world around her. She needed newness and wholeness and a different life altogether. Her fearless persistence should not be overlooked as she made her way through the crowd.

Read Matthew 5:17, 26:2; 2 Corinthians 5:21; Ephesians 1:4, 7, 2:4; 1 John 1:17

What happened was her need outweighed her fear and she moved through this huge crowd, pushing and touching, as an unclean woman. She didn't care. She wanted her life back, to belong again. He was her last resort and little did she know, all she would ever need. Her urgency is tangible. The Gospel of Mark gives us a little more detail when he adds that when she heard about Jesus she *knew* if she just *touched His clothes* she would be healed. *She knew it.* To know is to believe, and as we see at the end, Jesus tells her that this is what has healed her. She didn't understand it. How or why. But she believed, and her faith had healed her. She didn't shout His name or grab His arm. The Gospel of Matthew details that she *"touched the edge of his robe"* (9:20). Many artists have successfully portrayed her actions as she reached for Jesus' hemline. Her weak and feeble hand came out from the bottom of the crowd, reaching for the slightest edge of Jesus' robe. One such painting I came across by accident on a trip to Magdala in Galilee. I was completely taken aback as I came around a corner and was unexpectedly met with the woman I had grown so fond of. Her likeness reveals the moment this supernatural event would take place and makes her relatable to all who had lost and had been found. This is symbolic and important to this lesson. Numbers 15:38-39 explains the significance of the hem or *fringe* of a man's robe. This requirement is specific to the daily remembrance of God's laws and command-ments and is a common sight in the Jewish community today. As this tassel or fringe sways, the wearer can not help but catch its movement and remember the holiness of God as they minister throughout the community. The bleeding woman *believed* that by simply touching Jesus' hem specifically, the purification and wholeness she so desperately sought would be transferred to her, and she was right.

Jesus' response to her touch is almost comical as He seeks to find the culprit. There were hundreds of peo-ple surrounding Him. Who touched Him? Even Peter questioned it. But what He says next is so telling. Jesus replies, "*Someone touched me. I know that my power has left me.*" He felt His healing power leave Him and she felt it enter her. She felt her own healing. She knew the minute she touched Him that she was different. He met her where she was, in all her uncleanliness, and washed her white as snow. Jesus' own power, resurrecting power, was now coursing through her being. What an example of forgiveness and restoration. Our rock-bottom need for Him compels us to the smallest part of Him, and His love and forgiveness fill us to the brim. A single touch, a simple prayer, and an open heart of infantile faith are all it takes for Him to turn to us and release all that He is over and through us.

As 21st-century people, we think that if we have health, wealth, and all things comfortable, then we must be doing something right. Therefore God is happy, and we are blessed. But as long as we are blessed, our quiver is full, our health is on point, and the picket fence is standing upright, then we really need for nothing. We can finally put our feet up and coast our way to the finish line. But what about those who are suffering? Is that for people who are not really paying attention? The deserving? The faithless? In John 9, the story of the blind man's parents who must surely have been sinners or why else would he have been born without sight? Even today there is a stigma where all the self-righteous look down upon the suffering with a "God bless" and a hope that it all works out.

I truly believe that the bleeding woman wouldn't give up a day of those 12 years for anyone's picket fence. It takes a lot of time and God's amazing grace to come to that place, but when we do come face to face with Jesus and see the results of our sorrow and suffering and the bigger purpose over our simple need for calm and okay, can we actually agree with it. And even then, we might not actually see it clearly, but we accept it in light of the bigger picture of God's will and way. Newly healed and resting in Jesus, the bleeding woman wouldn't have it any other way.

It doesn't always have to be the darkest valley or the highest mountain experience; it is only a decision to trust God with your life. The fact that we are still standing upright and walking with any kind of composure is enough for others to see that God's grace is sufficient. Keeping in perspective that we have a Creator God who knows and sees and wants nothing but our good. True good. Good that is heavenly but does not fit in with the status quo of the here and now. He hates our heartbreak and the sin of the world that stirs it up but is always ready to make new. And never to return us back to the way we were but better than we could have ever imagined and closer to Him, only to glorify His name in all we do going forth.

The bleeding woman experienced God's grace first-hand on that day she was healed. Her ailment was the only path to discovering Him. I have found myself waiting and longing to be through the struggle, to see the light. But I have discovered that once I reach for Him, my circumstances grow exceedingly dim, and it is only the light that I can now focus on.

Suffering and pain come in all levels. What breaks me might not be what breaks you. And then, of course, life just enters in. There is evil on this earth and it takes over sometimes. We can't explain its timing or its choice. But the only way to rise above it is with the grace of God. Even then, it might take a while to see His light. It doesn't mean that we walk away untouched and unscathed. There may be scars and holes that will remain. We don't just move on or get over it. Loss and trauma, pain and defeat, don't vanish into thin air. But we learn to trust God with all that we are. Like the bleeding woman, we must. He is all that she had and all that she needed. We may depend on ourselves or other healing elements until we finally choose to reach for Him through the crowd. When we finally do, we will realize that we were being pulled in by His love the whole time. It is then we receive his power. His peace. His unconditional love. It will flow through us like it did in the bleeding woman and we can step back into our place in this world. Better. Stronger. Whole in and through Him.

Remember *"rest in the land"*? This lines up well with our talk about healing. Luke's restoration stories represent God's restorative plan through Jesus, and we see that when God promised Israel a special land with rest. A place of safety and security in the presence of their

God. God was restoring Israel to their rightful place. A place of community and fellowship. A place of worship and wholeness. God gave the bleeding woman rest. That is what He gives His people. Healing. Restoration. Rest. I am not looking at suffering or loss as a "lesson to be learned" or "how God works" but as an assurance of God's presence right in the midst of it, pulling you close. I read a story recently that in the Garden of Eden, joy was the conduit that brought mankind into close fellowship with God. There was no darkness there. No sin, destruction, or pain. Their hearts were full of all that was necessary for goodness and peace. All the time. We were meant to walk in gratefulness and blessedness there with Him. But after the Fall, it would be sorrow and brokenness that would cause us to come to Him. Knowing our own loss of life, need for forgiveness, and restoration would one day cause us to push through the crowd at the answer standing before us. Although there is no Eden on earth at the moment, God is waiting to bring you back to lush ground. He is always using life as we know it to bring us to life as He created it to be. He will get us through the trauma and the scars left behind. He is waiting to lay us down in green pastures and bring us to calm waters so that we can take a breath and enter into His land of restoration. All we have to do is reach for Him.

TIME OF REFLECTION

- Think of the time you were healed, physically and spiritually.
- What did you rely on to get you through those times?
- How did God raise you up and restore you?
- What do you understand about yourself/God today after going through these trying times?
- What resonates with you most about the story of the bleeding woman? Most challenging?
- Think of the time you asked God for forgiveness and restoration. Write it down.

SCRIPTURAL PRAYER: *For he will deliver the needy who cry out, the afflicted who have no one to help. He will take pity on the weak and needy and save the needy from death. He will rescue them from oppression and violence, for precious is their blood in his sight. (Psalm 72:12-14)*

PERSONAL PRAYER: *Father in Heaven, heal me. Physically, emotionally, and spiritually. Bring me to the foot of the cross so that I might express all that I am to You. Help me, Lord, to bring it all to You. My suffering, my loss, my loneliness, my sin. Thank You, for sending Your Son to die for me. Thank You that I no longer walk in darkness because You have called me into the light. The light of Your presence is the only place I want to be. Help me to walk daily in the land that You have called me to and to receive the rest it offers. I am healed and whole. You have raised me to new life, restored me to a new family, and made me righteous in the eyes of God. Thank You, Jesus.*

CHAPTER SEVEN

WOMEN WHO WORSHIP

༄

C. S. LEWIS KNEW how to tell a story. He knew how to tell a story without telling you a story. I mean that's a thing right now. Social media puts a question out often for followers to tell them something without telling them exactly. But you always get it. This is C. S. Lewis' style. In his Chronicles of Narnia book, *The Lion, the Witch, and the Wardrobe,* he tells of the gentle yet commanding Lion of Judah who has come to defend his people in the land of Narnia and ultimately, to sacrifice his life to the evil Ice Queen in order to save the life of Prince Edmund, a wayward son. Tell me about Jesus without telling me about Jesus. Now I have several movies that render me to tears. I can sometimes just see the name of it and I know I will cry if I tune in. But Aslan in Narnia takes me to a whole new level. The scene of his violent death at the hands of the queen's evil monsters is hard for me to watch, but when Aslan rises again, over that broken slab with a mighty roar, well, it gets me every time. Every. Time.

I am a visual person, and even though I believe Jesus is my Savior through word, preaching, and personal experience, this picture just seals it even more. This scene is a reminder to me that I serve a mighty God. One who jumps to my defense from the daily evils that attack me inside and out, and especially against the one who comes for God's world as a whole. These mental pictures show us who our mighty and majestic Savior is and why He so deserves our full and undivided adoration and worship. The Lion of Judah is first spoken of in Genesis 49:8-12 and subsequently in Revelation 5:5, which foretells the future ruling king, a descendant from the Tribe of Judah, who will be victorious in His everlasting reign over His people. This prophecy gives us the promise of our Savior as we await in hope for the ultimate deliverance of His people. This hope emboldens me with His fierceness to take on the battle and know that I will win, or better yet, I already have. The one and only battle that makes me a true soldier in God's kingdom. In 1 Timothy 6:12, Paul's friend and traveling companion recognizes this battle as "the good fight," which does not involve a physical battle at all. Instead, it calls for a steadfast mind and an active life of faith, shrouded with obedience, along with a huge dose of humble servitude.

Just as Jesus declares in Luke 22 that servanthood is the greatest place in His kingdom, we see this fulfilled by faithful women who have followed Jesus to the very end of His life on earth. Their devotion to God comes through in their service to their Savior and ultimately to His people. In addition to being called to follow Christ, as His present-day disciples, we are also called to bring others along with us. We can worship God in many ways, through prayer, song, and offerings, but it comes full circle when we open the doors for others. As servants of God's kingdom, Paul tells us that first, we must *"imitate Christ's humility"* (Philippians 2:1-11). This involves bringing ourselves to a place of comfort and encouragement by remembering who created us and for what purpose. Surrendering to our place and position of God's call in this world, just as Jesus did, brings about the tenderness and compassion needed in order to pour out God's love onto others. Jesus Himself, as the Son of Man, combats any confusion among the disciples about His earthly mission when He clarifies that He came *"not to be served but to serve others, and to give His life as a ransom"* (Matthew 20:28). His instruction to His disciples becomes even clearer when He specifies that *"those who truly believe in me will do the works I am doing and they will do even greater things than these."* (John 14:12-14). As co-creators made in His image, this is what faithful believers are called to do.

In this chapter, we experience this type of humility as we see these women surrender their lives, showing proof of their identity as their faith is called into action. This last group of women in the gospel of Luke do not have prominent names or achieve any amazing feats, but they do play a significant role in the promotion of Jesus' mission on earth. Because of their newfound freedom in Jesus, these women have found their place by simply walking alongside Him, securing God's mission a success. These women blessed Jesus and His disciples with financial, emotional, and spiritual support. They were fierce enough to run ahead, walk beside, and bring up the rear in their quest to bring our Lord and Savior to the world. The women in these stories weren't just determined to do something good, but they were led by gratitude for what Jesus had personally done for them and what He was doing for the entire world. Sharing their God-given strengths, attributes, and even possessions for the cause of His kingdom became a form of worship, and their worship became a testimony for others to see. Their dedication, generosity, and heartfelt tears were evidence of their love and adoration for the One who came to serve and save the world.

THE WOMEN WITH THE OIL

The pouring of oil, particularly over the head, is an ancient tradition that is an act of acknowledgment and reverence to the great kings of the day. We see this play out in 2 Kings 9:6 when Elisha calls for the anointing of Jehu as the next King of Israel who will ultimately wipe out the wicked King Ahab, his wife Jezebel, and all of their descendants. In the same way, Jesus, the King of all kings, deserved this display of adoration like none other as He came to deliver the world from this same evil fate.

For clarity's sake, let me state that there are several "anointing oil" stories in the gospel that have a lot of similarities, and if not for timing and geography, we could easily lump them all together as one event. But although they have common elements, we are shown, by Jesus Himself, that these "anointings" differ in their purpose, and each sheds light on Jesus' sacrificial call and compassionate nature.

In Luke 10, we are introduced to Martha and Mary in Bethany, preparing a dinner to honor their guest of honor, Jesus. Every woman who has ever studied the Bible is most likely well aware of this heated debate between Mary, the studious listener, and her hardworking sister, Martha. Their names also appear in John 11 when Jesus raises their brother Lazarus from the dead. But most importantly, we find in Matthew 26, Mark 14, and John 12 that this same Mary is the woman who pours oil on Jesus at a dinner in Bethany at the onset of Passion Week. Although these stories differ in various details, Matthew and Mark report that she actually poured it over His head as He reclined at the table. This detail helps in securing her purpose when Jesus rebukes the disciples' disgust at the waste of it all and explains her intentions to prepare His body for burial and His soon departure from them. What Mary shows here is her complete faith in the Messiah's true mission and the purpose of the sacrifice that He has come to accomplish. The sweet, satisfying aroma of her purifying act would fill the room, covering the rising haze of death as she publically set Jesus apart as the Redeemer and placed Him one step closer to God's salvific plan. Mary's choice of the "better things" has awarded her with a deep understanding that identifies Jesus as the one and only King of kings.

The nameless "sinful" woman found in Luke 7:36-50 takes place in Galilee early on in Jesus' ministry and occurs for a completely different reason as Jesus, again, explains. As Jesus dined with a Pharisee, the woman gained entrance into the male-dominated dinner and positioned herself at His feet, pouring the perfume over them, wiping it with her hair, and kissing them all while she wept. She had learned that Jesus was there and came prepared with her aromatic anointing oil to show her gratitude for the forgiveness He bestowed on her. Jesus explains that the "sinner" has chosen not His head to ordain Him king but His feet to show her great love and devotion for her Savior who has washed her white as snow.

Both of these Marys came prepared to meet Jesus and to bestow on Him their heartfelt desire to publicly recognize their Messiah and Savior. Determined to show Him and those watching how their lives had changed since coming face to face with the One who saves and forgives. They brought with them the best they could offer: their gifts, sweet and aromatic, poured out over Him. Their actions proved their devotion to Jesus and a desire to show it to the world. They were no longer steeped in the weight of the world but were now led by the desire to live a life of worship and servitude to a much greater reality.

Through the example of these two women, we are able to see what our true purpose is through a deep relationship with our Savior. When we discover who He is and why He came, our direction and focus are greatly altered. No longer is the fulfillment of earthly desires at the forefront of our lives nor is the seeking of others' approval. When, like these Marys, we grasp the overwhelming feeling of gratitude as recipients of the precious gift of salvation, our lives are redirected to the servant's call that beckons us to share it with the world. From this change in our lives and hearts, we sense a call that is deeper than the outer workings of daily life. This call comes in the form of a simple gesture, word, or deed that reveals our true adoration to the One who calls. A talent, a specific ability, a gift that naturally flows once unleashed by the Spirit of God upon our agreement that we have been empowered to not live this life in vain.

THE WOMEN WHO GAVE IT ALL

In the first story that we see in Luke 21, Jesus compares the gifts of the rich to those of a poor widow. The widow, in contrast to the partial gifts of those much wealthier, gave all that she had as her temple offering. Jesus uses this story to show the difference between one who holds back with their best to a faithful believer who trusts God with all that they are and all that they have. The widow's denial of herself showed not only her complete devotion to her Savior but to His mission at large, which glorifies the Father. Her gift would allow Jesus' call to further reach others as He had obviously reached her. This shows how our faithfulness and complete trust in Jesus Christ move us compassionately to pay it forward. The call of the generosity of our time, money, or talents will naturally pour from us for His greater purpose once we begin to trust Him completely.

In just a few short sentences in Luke 8:1-3, we find more women who have chosen to support Jesus and His twelve disciples as they walked from town to town— healing, ministering, and offering the good news of the arrival of God's kingdom to the gathering crowds. These women had been healed, cured not just from bodily ailments but from "evil spirits and diseases," the scripture specifies. We are introduced to these women, Mary Magdalene, Joanna (the wife of a political official of Herod), Susanna, and others, for the purpose of showing their generosity, which would come from their own personal means. This, of course, could mean financial, but I have an idea that they gave whatever was at their fingertips. Like the poor widow, their generosity came from the personal touch of Jesus into their lives. Lifted from oppression and defeat, they heard, believed, and were changed by His healing hand, inwardly and outwardly. An innate call to surrender, not just themselves, but all they had to Him and for Him.

This call to give, to surrender, should come naturally as we realize our need for Him and for all that He has done for us. The true acknowledgment of His death for our sins, His healing of our deepest wounds, and His resurrection which takes us to new life with Him, leads us to a higher playing ground. One that looks above the chaos of this world and into the heart of God's people. Where generosity of gifts, whatever they may be, are used for a higher calling than just good deeds or works. This type of generosity, one for the kingdom of God, for the purpose of Jesus' mission, is one that freely flows from our hands and our hearts because we have experienced Him at the deepest level.

THE WOMEN WHO FOLLOWED

At the end of Jesus' life, we find this same group of women keeping watch closely over Jesus' every move. They are careful not to interfere but to watch from afar as He walks toward the purpose for which He came. Although these women are referred to mostly as the "women who came with Him from Galilee," we find in Matthew 27:55 that these women include Mary (Mother of James and Joseph) and the mother of Zebedee's sons as well as several unnamed followers. In contrast to the women of Jerusalem who, Luke 23 writes, after gathering at the sight of the cross, mourned and wailed and then went away, these strong and devoted women who had followed Him from Galilee, and all those who "who knew Him," stood at a distance, watching it all. Calmly taking it in. As if they knew it had to be done. They knew and had understood as a united community of believers what Jesus had come to do. No tears or hysterics could change or would change this course in history. They continued to follow to the tomb where He was being taken and back the next day to prepare His body with spices for proper burial. Their diligence and faithfulness allowed them to be the first to find an empty tomb where God's purpose and plan became perfectly clear.

Let me add here that I am in awe of these women. I probably shouldn't be, knowing that this type of faith is not innate but given by the Spirit simply by the desire to know our Father. The devotion that emanates from them makes me seek more and more to be known in this way. To never show defeat or loss even in the darkest days because my faith has guaranteed me so much more than this present moment. To be so strong in my own redemption journey that gratitude and humility will cause me to wait when needed and persevere when called. To calmly take the steps needed to make sure our Savior is known and His identity cared for is something that we all should crave from the hillside.

These women followed Jesus from beginning to end. This was not just a solitary, extraordinary event that happened in their life or a momentary revelation. They were changed forever. They believed, remembered, and remained faithful until the end and beyond. In their worship of the true Messiah, they gave themselves completely: their time, their resources, their devotion. They used whatever they had to show their love and faith in God's mission for the salvation of the world, and they joined Him in moving it forward. They received and they gave back because this is what true worship and gratitude of our Savior looks like. It comes from the heart and it flows to the world. This is discipleship at its best and is an example that leads us to discover ourselves and our place in this amazing journey above and beyond our worldly existence.

Read 1 Samuel 12:24, John 12:26, Romans 12:1, Hebrews 9:14

May we begin to see the Bible as an open-ended reflection of the needs of ALL God's people so that we might realize the empowerment that comes from God's present love for each and every one of us. Let us embrace our individualism as it pertains to God's particular call and gifting so that it may be useful inside and outside the community. Now that we have been empowered with everything we need to walk out this spiritual life, let's dig a little deeper within to find our own personal call.

FINDING YOU

Although Hamlet's words "to thine own self be true" can take on multiple meanings, ownership of one's self is what pops into my mind. To know who you are and why you are here is essential in narrowing down our spiritual purpose and calling. Just like any worldly occupation or career, we have to be equipped to find our created place in this world. But since God has already equipped us in every way, it is now our time to receive it. Knowing the truth about who we really are, being still, and listening to what God is trying to reveal to us is what lands us in the right place.

The word "calling" means to have *a strong inner impulse toward a particular course of action, especially when accompanied by conviction of divine influence.* I think that sums up our mission in the kingdom of God. Because of your dependent, sold out, or shall I say *fierce faith,* in the amazing event of Jesus' death and resurrection, you now have the opportunity to worship Him through a personal ability given to you simply for this purpose. No matter where this ability or desire leads you, out in front of many or behind closed doors, it is our responsibility as part of this divine family, known better as "the body of Christ," to make the good news of Jesus available to all. Our resurrection to new life with Christ is what we are *called* to be witnesses to in one way or another. The one directive that stands out among the many is Jesus' commission in Matthew 28:19 to *"go and make disciples."* This is our purpose. This is why we were created. This is what our fierce faith emboldens us to do.

This week I want to start by helping you recognize what gifts and talents God has given you and help you hone into what it is that He has set apart for you. Our worship of God is not meant to turn our lives upside down but to bloom where we are standing. He calls us to take a step forward—to Him and our purpose. He is not calling us (or most of us) to travel the world or change our trajectory. He is simply saying to let it flow out right where you are. The attributes that we have been given to follow His lead are natural to our character and personality yet are for His great purpose. They are a part of who we were created to be, and through our identity in Christ, will become as natural as taking a breath. Discovering ourselves and the opportunities available to us makes the possibilities endless as we begin to walk in the land set before us. Our calling is something uniquely specific that connects us to kingdom life and for the greater good of all and is an outward revelation of our worship for Him. It is not something that is always easy on our part, and in fact, might be extremely uncomfortable at times, but it will and has always been for God's glory in us and through us. If we are seeking to find our place in God's realm, then maybe we should take a step back and evaluate some things about ourselves that God has been waiting to reveal.

To those who have said yes to His call, Jesus promises in this same verse that He is with us now and always will be. So, all that to say, when will you feel confident enough to believe you are chosen, called, loved, and completely able to accomplish what is in your heart? So ask yourself, what is in your heart? We can dream about being something, but is it really that out of the question? Do you have what it takes to actually make that thing happen? God is the equipper, but we are the body. We have to be the ones to own it and step into it. We have been supernaturally reinstated, but He has given us a brain. We have intellect and common sense. We are able because God said it so. It is noted in 2 Peter 1:3-9 that we are now *"partakers of the divine nature"* and because of this great gift we need to *"make every effort"* to add to it. Peter reminds us that we have everything, as laid out in Genesis 1, in order that we might *increase!* So we must keep moving, pressing forward to grow our faith. Becoming fierce and unwavering in confirming our call. Stepping out into our abilities and gifts so that we become a viable part of God's purpose to *"keep us from being ineffective and unproductive."*

Never forget that we are His co-creators, made in His image to increase, manage, and subdue (Gen. 1:26). From the first days of the world, we have been set apart to continue what God began. We have been given "everything" we need to move His creation forward. Like the women at the cross, let nothing hinder you from seeing His mission fulfilled, eager to share the news with those nearby. We, too, have been called to be this type of discipleship. We have been given certain personalities, gifts, and abilities that are meant solely for this purpose and to see it through in our lifetime.

FINDING YOUR PLACE

First, let's get a few things out of the way. Sometimes I think we get misdirected or confused about what kinds of "good stuff" we should be doing. There always seems to be a job that needs to be done at all levels of the church, community, and spiritual business. As servants to God, it is our responsibility to fill this never-ending list that keeps His kingdom on its feet. There isn't a position or place in the church that is better than another, and everything the body is called to do is *GOOD*. But if you are just doing things to be doing them or following the crowd to stay relevant, then read on.

It is in our human nature to be needed and known for something. None of us want to live this life in vain. Being a part of something valuable is in our DNA. That desire was put there by God who created us for just a time as this. But unfortunately, this is what drives us to grasp any and all opportunities because, for the most part, they are all good. We are born with the desire to belong to something good and to leave behind a legacy that says we did what we needed to do. So if that is true, what is wrong with randomly choosing something "good" to do in the church or community? In other words, let me fill up my time chasing after random projects because it's good instead of letting God show me what has specifically been set apart for me and actually making a difference in the kingdom of God so that I can be exactly what God created me to be. Huh? So that's a thing, is it??

It is easy to see what someone else is doing and to just follow their path. They look so happy and comfortable, and you just know that you will feel the same way if you do what they are doing. But honestly, that never works out for very long as most of us who have tried it can tell you. So when do we ever sit down and think about who we are and what our true purpose is? When do we stop and simply ask God what He wants of us? This is key to knowing where we best fit, where we will do our best work, and namely, where God will be glorified at every turn. You see, that's the big picture. If we are not first doing this for God and His big-picture kingdom plans, then we might as well not waste our time. You might be making someone happy temporarily, but you are doing nothing for their eternal soul, not to mention missing the very people God has purposefully put in your path. You will ultimately get worn out, frustrated, and completely bored with making someone else's calling yours. So let's start that true-to-self thing here.

In order to find out what our kingdom qualities are, sometimes they have to be unearthed. This is where God will keep turning you back around to the same lessons over and over again until you finally begin to see things His way. The way that will fulfill and complete you and yes, again, glorify His name. Maybe for some, they knew at the age of five what they were supposed to be and never veered off course. For me...uh no. It seems as if I had to choose the hardest way possible in order to find my way back, but praise the Lord, I always did find my way back. Suffering, failure, and hardship are not anything I wished upon myself, but it is the very thing that "unearthed" who I really am. First Peter 5:10 ensures that *"the God of all grace, who called you to his eternal glory in Christ, after you have suffered a little while, will himself restore you and make you strong, firm and steadfast."* I can look back now at the arduous situations and events that arose in my life and see how much God was pressing in on me to let it all go. I have felt His presence literally sitting on me until I waved the white flag of surrender. Sometimes our feathers have to be ruffled in order to lose a few top layers. I sometimes think that we focus so much on the blessings and peace in our life, that we forget that our discomfort and sacrifices are required for our spiritual maturity.

I am one of those believers who has been guilty of seeking peace and comfort as if it was actually a destination in the Christian life. If I can prove to other believers that I have checked all the boxes, that I have achieved all that is achievable, and that God has *"blessed"* me because look how comfortable and perfect my life is...well then, I have totally missed the boat on all things pertaining to spiritual growth and discipleship. Even though 1 Peter 5:6-7 promises humbled leaders they will one day be *"exalted,"* our calling is never what is in it for me. It is hard work and flesh-eating stuff, not for the faint of heart. It is for those who are willing to be made tough enough to endure what you have to endure to make sure His name is spoken and remembered. The goal is to use our calling as humble servants of God and of others. The true exaltation comes just by knowing these two factors have been accomplished; everything else is filler. So before we go building a tower with our name on it, let's keep our focus on who truly deserves to be exalted.

It is time for some self-awareness that helps us critique our strengths and weaknesses, dreams and desires, and gifts and talents so that we can present them as sacrifices for God's glory. Here is what is funny. You already know. What is in the back of your head just needs to be pulled to the front. Time to clean out the junk so that it has room to come through. Remember the land and the rest in the land. Remember the bleeding woman who was filled with His power. That belongs to us too. You already have everything residing in you that you need to be all of you. You have just got to clear out the muck covering it up. Oh, wouldn't it be nice to let all that stuff go that I have built up in my head? And oh, how we can do that, can't we? Speculations, ruminations, fears, opinions, and judgments just run rampant in our heads. But what if we just let it go, I mean, really *LET IT GO.* Just a giant eraser wiping it clean. Replacing those things with a focus on God, His Word, His great plan and purpose in my life, and just to walk in that and let Him take care of all the world stuff swirling around me. Remember that little ditty in Philippians 4:6? "Don't be anxious for anything." Take it for its true meaning—let it all go.

Now there will be circumstances and people that seem to bring out the worst in us. As hard as you try to wean yourself from destructive situations, they seem to keep showing up uninvited. It will seem like the same events or relationships just keep happening. In my experience, I realized that I was the common denominator, and God in His loving way was simply bringing to the surface what needed to be exposed. He was faithfully pruning me of attitudes, expectations, and judgments in order to replace them with acceptance and forgiveness of others and of myself. He just kept bringing it all back around until I saw the light. I needed to quit trying to change what was around me and focus on the only thing I could change—me. God allows disruption and disturbance in our lives to basically wear us out in battle. To stop putting up a fight. To stop trying to win or seek vindication. He wants us to surrender it all, sit at His feet, and soak it all in. He wants us to be a Mary, still and quiet and listening to Him. He wants us to rest in the land and let Him fight the battle. He wants us to just walk in Him. He is washing off of you the ability to let anything that is in or of this world affect you. He is pouring out compassion, mercy, and just plain old goodness over us. I have had to back up after many years of being worried about the events around me and what others might be doing to simply trust God with every part of my being. He circumvents all people, places, and things that try to interrupt my trust in Him; I simply have to remain in that trust. When I remain faithful to my purpose and place in His great creation, I am automatically front and center within His will. I become untouchable, unchangeable, and unmovable, just like flint.

WHAT DO YOU WANT?

The story of the paraplegic man in John 5 always rocks my boat. Jesus comes upon a paralyzed man lying on a mat and lamenting the fact that he can't get into the water to be healed fast enough. Someone always beats him to it and gets the healing first. Now there are numerous lessons that we can get from this story but the one that fits here is that Jesus basically asked the man, "What do you want?" This is key to what I am saying here. God has given us everything to do what we need to do. Remember…His image, co-creators. We were set up to win from the beginning. He has given us abilities, He has given us dreams and desires, and in this story we see Him tell this man to *take his mat and walk.* Get up and go after what you want. Tapping into our personal dreams and desires is a slippery slope that needs to be tread on with spiritual shoes. So when we begin to look at what is on our hearts and minds, we always need to look at it from a spiritual perspective and how it will benefit the kingdom of God. So what I need for you to do here is to begin to think about what you are thinking about. When you see yourself out in the world, where are you standing? I mean, what do you want? For instance, do you see yourself standing on a stage leading a crowd or back behind a curtain running the show? Your thoughts are indicative of what is in your heart, and as humans, there are plenty of thoughts that can waste our time, but beneath all of that is the truth. Anything where you see yourself most likely is showing you something that you were meant to be. Leaders are born, it has been said, but you have to make your way to the front of the line. All this to say, your thoughts and desires are telling you what is in your heart. Fear of failure or thoughts of unworthiness are the only things standing in your way. I have had both and they are roadblockers and time-wasters for sure. If you are thinking there is truth in it somewhere, ask God to show you where to use it. Ask for an opportunity as well as confirmation that reveals your true created self.

But there is another side too. How about never, ever doing anything wrong? Staying so tied to the pier for fear of sinking that you best not even try. I know that feeling personally. Being paralyzed by fear is Satan's best weapon to make sure you do nothing for the kingdom of God. You might believe that someone else will do it better, which might be true, but what does that matter? God's truth is God's truth and there is no bad way to share it. So instead of keeping it safe and pretending it's all okay, you miss your call and the people meant to be blessed by your gifts. There is the bondage of living in sin, and there is the bondage of trying to be perfect. Neither one is good. Let your guard down. Fearing what people might think or say is making them an idol in your life. I have to fight that fear daily as I put these words on paper and think of where it all leads. Am I ready, worthy, or able? Yes, I am, because God has made it so. So please don't put man's opinion over God's call; it is defeating, has no purpose, and is breaking the first commandment, so let's not start with a negative.

Although God provided every word and motivation behind every single thing that I wrote or spoke, it took a while before I grasped the whole concept of what I was actually doing. When I first began to teach, I was literally a nervous wreck. It might not have shown outwardly but inside, for days before I had to stand before those sweet young married faces, I was a mess. I fretted and perfected my lesson and fretted some more. I actually could not eat in the days leading up to Sunday morning. I would drive myself to church, alone, because I couldn't bear conversation to interrupt my paranoia. Then one Sunday morning as I presented my carefully crafted and perfectly coiffed lesson, the unthinkable happened. I lost my place. Now everyone who has ever spoken in public knows, this is the nightmare that makes us sit straight up in bed. Besides walking down our high school halls unclothed, this is the dream that sends us into shivers. I. Lost. My. Place. My perfectly lined-up notes got out of order, I lost control of what I worked hard to control, I lost control of myself, and I stammered and stuttered, trying to regain my composure. I am still not sure how I pulled it back together or even if I did, but I beat myself up the whole day, and it took me a week to get it out of my mind. But now I know that this is the best thing that could have ever happened. Exhausted and frustrated, I begged God to let me stop, let me out...take this cup! But the Spirit led me to say these words to my sweet Father in heaven who knew me so well. I asked that God would "let me love it or let me go," and He said so sweetly and parentally..."Then take your eyes off yourself." Gulp. You see, I fretted and perfected and fretted some more because I cared so much, too much, about what everyone was thinking about ME! Uh, not God or His Words or their salvation, but myself. I let go right there. I asked for forgiveness and I surrendered it all. Every word, every person, and every lesson going forward! All yours, God. Get me out of the way. I was delivered that day and I never looked back. I studied, I taught it, and I went home. I stopped critiquing every word and grading myself every Sunday. What a weight lifted off of me. It was about God the whole time. I became invisible, and I had never been happier. Let me add to this overly dramatic story that is my middle name, that no one cared. This room was, first, filled with people who were not called to teach nor did they want to. So hearing someone mess up was hardly something they judged because they were just glad they were not up there to begin with and because they loved me, and I am sure it was probably pretty entertaining to watch me completely wig out.

So begin today to ask yourself (and God) who you really are. Do you want to know your real purpose? Are you willing to listen to the Spirit who is searching your heart to reveal what's in there? Are you ready to be peeled back to receive what is yours? Paul emphasizes in Philippians 3:12-14 the one thing he does to *"take hold of that for which Jesus Christ took hold of me."* What Jesus had called him to. Held over him that gave him the drive and devotion to start and finish the task. The desire, not to just work at it, but to *"take hold"* of it. Make it his. All his, without doubt of any ability of his own but in knowing that God will see it through. Paul continues that *"forgetting what is behind and straining toward what is ahead,"* he pushes *"forward to the goal to win the prize for which has* called *me heavenward in Christ Jesus."* He keeps moving toward it. He feels the weight of the call. The importance of its delivery. The consequences of its incompleteness. He knows he must keep on. This is a call, not a "good" job to be done because we are something special. It will work because we are all sinners saved by grace and because of that, we can openly and freely preach the gospel with all confidence in the knowledge that we are His for this purpose and for this purpose alone.

The women who followed Jesus show us the determination and devotion that comes from realizing Jesus as our Savior and Messiah and the call that came upon their lives. Simply by His touch, they were restored to life. They were changed forever and dedicated their lives to giving all they had for God's salvific plan for creation. They walked with Him, letting nothing get in the way of their dedication to their great Savior. Their call to follow Him was the greatest form of worship. Even in the hostile world surrounding them, their fierce faith pushed past the doubt and gloom with all eyes on the One who was sent to defeat it all

TIME OF REFLECTION

- What have you discovered about your own personal salvation through this study? Where have you changed? What do you need to work on?
- How have you been encouraged by what Christ has done for you on the cross? How have you been comforted by the thought of His grand love for you? How have you been compelled to serve Him based on what He has done for you?
- Think about your gratitude for what God has done for you through Jesus Christ. Ask the Holy Spirit to help you understand the love of God that leads you to a thankful heart.
- Do you have a personal calling in God's kingdom? What are your *unique gifts*?

- Talents? Personal desires and abilities that could be or are being used to further God's kingdom purposes?
- What do you have that can be shared with others? How generous are you with what God has given you?
- What do you do that is supportive and encouraging others? Bringing others intothe community of believers and helping other believers? How are you stirring others up in the Lord? Who have you invited into the church community?
- What do you envision yourself doing or would like to be doing? Is God drawing you into a special place in His community? Just as Jesus asked the man at the pool, "What do you want?"

SCRIPTURAL PRAYER: *I keep asking that the God of our Lord Jesus Christ, the glorious Father, may give you the spirit of wisdom and revelation, so that you may know him better. I pray that the eyes of your heart may be enlightened in order that you may know the hope to which he has called you, the riches of his glorious inheritance in his holy people, and his incomparably great power for us who believe. That power is the same as the mighty strength he exerted when he raised Christ from the dead and seated him at his right hand in the heavenly realms, far above all rule and authority, power and dominion, and every name that is invoked, not only in the present age but also in the one to come. (Ephesians 1:17-23)*

PERSONAL PRAYER: *Unhinge me from this world and give me the courage to step out to find who I am and where I belong. Help me to connect my human-ness to Your di-vine-ness so that I may be used as Your arms and legs in this world. May I fall into the arms of the Spirit, Father, so that I might further Your kingdom by doing the good works that You created me to do. Help me to know myself as You know and love me, and direct me in all of Your ways. Renew me so that I might walk in fierce faith to bring in and build up Your body of believers. Thank You for your mercy and grace through the death and resurrection of Your Son, Jesus Christ, our Savior and Lord.*

CHAPTER EIGHT

WANTING MORE

೮૩

WALKING THROUGH THE stories of the Bible, I find a common denominator between some of the characters that we all know, love, and relate to. No matter who they were or what they had accomplished, they were driven by this deep inner desire for "more." At the time, they probably could not have even explained it, but they all just knew that there was something out there that they were supposed to have that went way beyond the moment, beyond materialism, and way beyond personal power and comfort.

WANT MORE

Once the invitation for more came, even in fear, lack of understanding, or their belief in their inability, Abraham and Moses humbly surrendered. Even when they balked and tried to walk away, something inside told them they couldn't. Hannah wanted more for Samuel, a baby that she had prayed for and anguished over and cried to the Lord for, but she still readily handed him over to Eli because she knew he was meant for more. In the book of John, although she had had five husbands and was presently living with a man, the Samaritan woman at the well was still thirsty, wanting more. The paralytic at the pool knew that in that swirling water, there was healing and he wanted it. He wanted more. But the story that speaks to me, is the story of David, a man who was created for "more." This is an age-old story that we all know well, heard lots of times in many different ways, but I love it because I relate to it, and I believe that this is exactly how God works in those who have been filled with the desire for "more."

David was anything but perfect, but his life is such an example of what God wants in those He has called. It is a story about the testing of character, of strength, of common sense, of faith, and especially a story that shows that God's people were meant for "more." In Acts 13:22, God tells Samuel, *"I have found David, son of Jesse, a man after my own heart; he will do everything that I want him to do."* I searched Scripture to find something about David's faithfulness to God as a young man or something that expressed his outward dependence on Him, but I didn't find anything that told me exactly what David had done or acted to prove to us that he was a man of fierce faith. So what was God seeing in David? Even though David is described as healthy, fine, and handsome like his predecessor, Saul, God would call Samuel to look deeper this time. God knew his heart and had been preparing him for this day. David had the lowest job possible as a shepherd. He spent his days and nights tending sheep, alone out in a pasture. But as we can see by looking backward in Scripture, God was with him. He was fine-tuning his musical skills that would come in handy in calming Saul's tormented mind, fine-tuning his bravery and courage against voracious animals because of the giants he would face in the future, fine-tuning his ability to herd large groups of sheep because of the kingdom he would one day rule. As we know now, not one moment was wasted. Although to the world it looked useless and mundane, David was unknowingly being prepared for *more.*

WAIT FOR MORE

David's story begins in 1 Samuel 16:10-12 after God's prophet rejects all his brothers as Saul's replacement as the next King of Israel. David's father, Jesse, sends for him to come in from the fields at Samuel's request, and is immediately declared as "the one." Hand-picked, chosen out of the crowd. The least and most unlikely. Of all Jesse's sons, God chose David. What a powerful example and a great reminder of how God works in the life of His people. David had a lot of time on his hands, and I am sure he thought about his life. I imagine he dreamed about his goals and desires, about what he wanted to be. Maybe he even thought about being a great leader. But even when they called him in from the fields he had no idea what was in store. Just like David, our journey for "more" is not always evident in our lives. You may be at the beginning of this journey of "more" and are most likely basing your future on where you are right now.

Maybe your abilities/degree/immediate desires have you looking ahead in speculation. But you really don't have any idea what that looks like. We don't know how it will turn out or what the twists and turns are, but we must stay focused on where we are in the present. We tend to focus on the big-ticket items of our life that we think will sell us and what we think God can use best. But based on David's story, a totally different thing happened. God used the practical, mundane, and basic human traits and talents to prepare him for greater things. David is out in the wilderness, a very lonely place, and his brothers are off being soldiers, fighting giants, and making Dad proud. But David is in the fields playing the flute, maybe to entertain himself or just for some noise in the darkness, or maybe just out of complete boredom, but what's crazy is his ability to play the flute was one of the things that opened up the doors. David was devoted to God, but it was God who was putting MORE into motion, not David. Right now, you are on the very cusp of the beginning of MORE. Don't overthink it. David wasn't thinking "Hey, if I play the flute or kill a lion, maybe I'll be the next King of Israel." He just did what he did. Just walk in it, and if you find yourself alone and in the wilderness, remain there until God sends for you. And remember, whatever happens in that wilderness, it is for His purpose to give you MORE.

RECEIVE MORE

The moment Samuel anointed David with oil, marking him as Saul's replacement as King of Israel, God's Spirit came "powerfully" upon him (1 Samuel 16:13). As we see with the women who anointed Jesus, David is sanctified, set apart as God's representative. The power of the Lord came upon him, and his *more* was put into action. His family watches, I am sure, in awe, as David receives his call and the oil is poured over him. He didn't question it or rebuke it. He didn't diminish his abilities or ask for a moment to think. He didn't see it as a choice between kingship and his life as it is. He took it as if he was expecting it all along.

As the youngest, born into dysfunction and divorce, my young life was founded on feelings of insecurity and unworthiness. Because of the void that comes with the lack of strong parental leadership and validity, I lived among the sheep in the wilderness for most of my young life. Even when blessings appeared and God opened doors, unlike David, I seemed to focus on what I didn't have instead of what He had graciously handed down to me. It wasn't until I was an adult that I remembered a voice speaking a promise over me when I was nine years old. At the time, the strong voice I felt and heard didn't make much sense to me and I soon forgot, but later as I began a deeper walk with God, I was reminded that it was Him all along. This was the beginning of my call for *more* that had been brewing in me for many years. I realized it had been buried under shame, guilt, and my own sin because I still believed only in my own unworthiness. As I reached out for certainty, I found Jesus who saved me and the Creator God who knew the true me. Through this foundational step, I learned to embrace the wilderness. The circumstances I was born into were now replaced with a new life and identity and could now be used to relate to those similar. I could now see the difference between a life living in past negativity compared to one of humble confidence blanketed in eternal hope.

See Ephesians 1:5-10

My journey of *more* began to move full-steam when I realized that I wasn't the person of my circumstances but who I was created to be. One of my favorite scriptures, Romans 8:37, sealed it for me as I came to the understanding that I am *"more than a conqueror."* I am not just to get over things or forget them. First, I am to forgive and let go, but I am also called to "take control of them." I learned to manage and subdue. I learned to check the old self and work to replace it with the new one. I sought to "increase" my faith, knowledge, and understanding and allowed God to bring me "more." I learned to sit still in the battle and seek the truth that resulted. I fought back the lies Satan continued to spew regarding my unworthiness and replaced them with the truth of God's Word that He had spoken over me.

In my journey for *more,* God called me exactly where I was but He didn't stop there. He created me to be exactly who He needed me to be but there was some fine-tuning to be done. I wasn't meant to have what anyone else had. I was meant for God's specific purpose. He had reached into my life very early and set me apart, and those feelings of difference had a purpose. They caused me to question and seek deeper things. Things that only God could and would answer.

Now this doesn't mean I don't still battle the sins of the past or face the scars of dysfunction that raise their ugly heads in an attempt to throw me off course. Oh, those things are there. They are part of me and will probably always come along for the ride. But the battle is the Lord's, and by knowing, not only this truth but the truth of who He is and who I am in Him, I can boldly face any of those past deterrents with a spirit of power and victory. So I don't have to tell you to seek out the invitation that God calls over you, because if you want more like David, you will wait for it. God is preparing you for it right now. You will know when the time is right and you will realize that you were expecting it all along. The day will come, an invitation will appear, a door will be opened, your journey for *more* will be confirmed, and there's a good chance you felt it all along.

BECOME MORE

Throughout the Bible, God renames His people: Abram to Abraham, Jacob became Israel, and who can forget Peter the Rock? In Acts 13, David's father had called him the younger, but God called him a king. Your name may sound the same but it has a whole new meaning once you begin to walk in "more." You are the same person, but now you belong to God and no one else. God is not trying to change you into something you are not. He is working to make you all that you already are. Your personality and natural characteristics are you...and that's what He wants. You.

I once heard someone say that David received a "miracle memory" when he left his old life for his new one. He did not forget his past but he did not look back as a victim, as insignificant, weaker, or less than. He looked back as a man who had been chosen by God to do great things. This means that we get to let go of all that might have been put on us, the rejection and other people's opinions of us, or any discouraging word that told us we weren't what God said we were. We can't move freely and purposefully in God's kingdom when we are wearing old, ragged, ill-fitting clothes that weren't meant for us to begin with. Wear your new name proudly. God's provision for your "more" is on repeat. As His good and faithful servant, God's more never ends. So wait patiently while God puts your new life into motion, extending your joy and giving your name a whole new meaning.

TIME OF REFLECTION

- Ask God to peel back the layers and reveal your true heart. What is your "more?" Be sincere in your desire to know Him and who you are in Him.

- Continue to release "busyness" to make room for "good works." Let go of the desire to be seen or known for the things of this world and to sit quietly in His presence.

- What is your heart speaking to you right now about your gifts and talents that will lend to the kingdom?

- Have you made the decision to be a living sacrifice for the Lord? To commit your life to His service? To let nothing hinder you from Him and His will for your life?

- Are you praying for fierce faith? Courage to step out and into His glory?

SCRIPTURAL PRAYER: *I always thank my God because of his grace given me in Christ Jesus. For in him I have been enriched in every way—with all kinds of speech and with all knowledge . . .Therefore, I do not lack in any spiritual gifts as I eagerly wait for the Lord Jesus Christ to be revealed. He will also keep me firm to the end, so that I will be blameless . . .God is faithful, who has called me into fellowship with his Son, Jesus Christ, our Lord. Amen. (1 Corinthians 1:4)*

PERSONAL PRAYER: *Heavenly Father, thank You for moving in my heart to bring me to Your will and calling in my life. I thank You that You have "more" for me than I could ever imagine. I receive all that You have and ask that You prepare me for this work. Let my life be an example to others and a refreshing aroma of the gospel to all those who are near me. May I always be courageous in doing Your will and not let anything hinder me from service to You and Your church. Amen.*

CONCLUSION

 R

MY HOPE IS that this study has helped you begin to find your fierce faith. My prayer is that God has brought you to these words and that they have resonated with your heart and mind. God has always been faithful to speak to me through other's writing. Besides His own Word, I have been blessed by many authors whose books have been supernaturally placed in front of me. Many times I have found exactly what I needed in someone else's wisdom that led me onward on my own personal path. Words that I knew God wanted me to hear and purposefully made available. They never failed to speak directly to my circumstances and to my call. My heartfelt desire is that I am able to pay it forward to you here.

I leave you with one question: Where are you? After going through these chapters and answering the questions regarding your personal salvation, and after evaluating your own God-given gifts and attributes, where are you? I invite you to continue to assess where these study questions have left you and better yet, where God is taking you. I hope you have begun to narrow down what truly it is that you want to do with what God has given to you. As you wait for His call and for those open doors, trust that He will surely provide. Let's not stop seeking Him, so you might present yourself fully mature in Christ in hopes of bringing others to the same result.

STAYING FOCUSED

1. Be Devoted to Prayer

Before running off and asking all your friends and family what you should do, take it before the Lord and then wait. Advice comes quickly, but God's instruction comes in His timing and is always perfect.

2. Read His Word

God wrote you a letter to tell you exactly who He was, is, and is to come.

Read it over and over. Commit yourself to daily Bible devotion and to the scriptural-based leadership of your church.

3. Be Obedient

When we choose the Lord as our personal Savior and trust God's Word for our lives, we have to be ready to obey. To go where He leads and let go of what He pulls us away from. Surrender it all as you trust God with your whole life.

4. Trust in the Lord's Strength

Choosing Jesus as our Savior is the last thing the enemy wants. Be ready and alert to his destructive and negative attacks as he attempts to turn you from God's purpose for your life. Remember who and whose you are. Give it to the Lord. The battle is His.

5. Always Be Fierce

You have everything you need to stand strong in the Lord. You are now able to boldly go before the throne of God. You are His child. Nothing can separate you from Him. Nothing you do, nothing anyone does to you.

You are now free to be the person He created you to be.

This Christian statement of faith originated in AD 325 at the Council of Nicea to address heretics who were misleading believers in the nature of the relationship between the Father and the Son. The creed confirms the faith of the Christian church.

THE NICENE CREED

We believe in one God, the FATHER, THE ALMIGHTY
maker of heaven and earth, of all that is seen and unseen.
We believe in one Lord, JESUS CHRIST, the only Son
of God, eternally begotten of the Father, God from God,
Light from Light, true God from true God.
Begotten, not made, one in Being with the Father.
Through him all things were made.
For us men and for our salvation He came down from
heaven; by the power of the Holy Spirit He was born
of the Virgin Mary, and became man.
For our sake he was crucified under Pontius Pilate;
he suffered, died and was buried.
On the third day he rose again in accordance with the
Scriptures; he ascended into heaven and is seated at the
right hand of the Father. He will come again in glory to
judge the living and dead.
And His kingdom will have no end.
We believe in the HOLY SPIRIT, the Lord, the giver of
life, who proceeds from the Father and the Son.
With the Father and the Son He is worshiped and
glorified.

He has spoken through the Prophets.
We believe in one holy catholic and apostolic church.
We acknowledge one baptism for the forgiveness of sins.
We look for the resurrection of the dead, and the life of
the world to come.

About the Author

CAROL TOWNSEND is a long-time Bible study teacher and a first-time author. She received her degree in Christianity from Houston Christian University in Houston, Texas, which led her to write this book. Carol wrote and teaches A *Walk Through the Bible Overview* in her home in Waco, Texas. She is an active member at Highland Baptist Church as well as on the the Board of Advocates for the School of Christian Thought at her alma mater. She has been married to Kirk for 33 years, and they have one daughter, Anna.

Sources

- Clairborne, Shane, Wilson-Hargrove, Jonathan, and Okoro, Enuma. "A Liturgy to Women," The Book of Common Prayer: A Liturgy for Ordinary Radicals (Grand Rapids: Zondervan, 2010), 562.
- Truth, Sojourner. "Anti-Slavery Bugle." Chronicling America. Accessed August 14, 2023. https://chroniclingamerica.loc.gov.
- Wright, N. T. "Women's Service in the Church: The Biblical Basis. A conference paper for the Symposium. 'Men, Women and the Church.' September 4, 2004. https://ntwrightpage.com.

Made in the USA
Monee, IL
20 January 2024